Defeating Your "Crazies"

Applying Cognitive Therapy Principles to Everyday Life Challenges

Richard Parsons Ph.D

outskirts
press

Outskirts Press, Inc.
http://www.outskirtspress.com

ISBN: 978-1-9772-1874-2

Outskirts Press and the "OP" logo are trademarks belonging to Outskirts Press, Inc.

PRINTED IN THE UNITED STATES OF AMERICA

Dedication

*To **YOU**, the reader, with the hope that you free yourself from the "big lie" and in so doing find a way to not only defeat your "crazies" but maintain your emotional well-being.*

Table of Contents

Acknowledgment

WHILE MY NAME is listed as the author of this book, the credit for its creation goes to the many therapists and researchers who have identified and refined our undertanding of the role that our thinking plays in the creation of our emotional upset. The work of scholar-practitioners such as Albert Ellis, Aaron Beck, and David Burns serves as the foundation to that which follows.

Besides these scholars, I wish to offer a heartfelt "thank you" to all of those individuals who, as clients in my private practice, invited me to walk with them during their times of struggle. My forty years as a psychologist in private practice has not only affirmed my belief in the strength of the human spirit, but it has also heightened my awareness of the power of our thinking in the creation and maintenance of our emotional well-being. I would also like to acknowledge the valuable work of my graduate assistant, Elizabeth Swierczek. Her suggestions increased the real-world applications of what is contained within this book.

Finally, to my wife, Ginny. Your editorial insights have

helped me craft the theory of cognitive psychology into a useful guide for each of us to follow. However, more than the sharing of your expertise, it is your sharing of unconditional love that makes all that I do possible.

rdp/2019

About the Author

THROUGH FORTY YEARS of teaching and the publication of more than eighty professional articles and books, Dr. Parsons has been able to contribute to the formation and training of numerous mental health specialists. In addition to his scholarly work, Dr. Parsons has engaged in clinical practice for over forty years, working with those experiencing debilitating anxiety, depression, and other challenges to their emotional well-being.

In this current book, he brings together his years of scholarship with his experience as a clinician to provide the reader with a well-researched, practical approach for navigating the demands of living in the twenty-first century and achieving an emotionally healthy life.

Introduction

*He is the most powerful who has power
over himself.*

Seneca (4 BC–AD 65)

HAVE YOU EVER been so angry you could just scream? How, about—has something ever scared the bejeezus out of you?

If you have ever encountered an intense negative emotion that not only disrupted your emotional well-being but may have taken form in some pretty useless (maybe even regrettable) behavior, then you came to the right place. KEEP READING!

Defeating Your "CRAZIES" Applying Cognitive Therapy Principles to Everyday Life Challenges is a book written for anyone who has ever found their peace of mind and emotional well-being disrupted by moments of anxiety, periods of anger or extreme annoyance, a sense of guilt, or other negative emotions. It is a book that will guide you in the development of a perspective and provide a set of skills that will help you maintain your emotional well-being even in light of the many daily challenges that you face.

A "Warning"

You should be warned, however, that this book and the perspective it offers brings with it some unique challenges. As you move through the upcoming pages, you will find that your fundamental view of yourself, others, and the world will be challenged. You may find that the perspective presented within this book is not only challenging but may even be a bit unsettling. But as you will quickly discover, embracing the perspective described and employing the skills presented will not only help you defeat your crazies but will result in your increased happiness and emotional well-being.

A Book for All of Us

In my years of clinical practice, I have been touched by my clients' experiences of complete hopelessness at the hands of depression; their inability to engage in life as they are frozen by the power of their anxiety; or their felt disempowerment at the hands of strong negative emotions.

Their experiences are dramatic and very sad. For example, there was Jan, a forty-two-year-old mother of three who found herself housebound due to her intense fear of being outside. There was William, a nineteen-year-old college student whose inability to tolerate minor frustration had led to multiple incidents of road rage. And finally, there was Elsa, a fourteen-year-old who in response to her experience of ongoing cyberbullying attempted suicide.

In working with my clients, I have employed a cognitive therapeutic approach—an approach with extensive research supporting its effectiveness in the treatment of depression, anxiety, stress, explosive anger, and other severe emotional difficulties. In addition to the value this approach has held for my clients, I have come to appreciate the fact that the principles and practices found in cognitive therapy have value for all people, not just those caught in the grips of severe emotional distress. Understanding and applying these principles and practices to your own life experiences will ensure your own increased happiness and emotional health and well-being.

Not Your Usual Self-Help Book

Defeating Your "CRAZIES" is not a typical self-help book. Yes, within the upcoming pages you will find concrete steps that will help you reduce the frequency and intensity of your disruptive emotions. However, what you will see in the pages **that follow** is more than a set of directives to use at moments of upset.

Defeating Your "CRAZIES" is a book that will invite you to change your fundamental perspective, beliefs, and assumptions about life and your response to it. This is a book that will help you gain a more rational view of life and life events and in so doing position you to not only maintain your emotional health and well-being but function more effectively.

So let's begin.

Let's begin to understand, attack, and ***Defeat Your "CRAZIES"!***

Rdp/2019.

CHAPTER 1

Our Crazies Start with Buying the BIG Lie

What upsets people are not things themselves but their judgments about things.
—Epictetus (ca. A.D. 50–130)

YOU'VE BEEN LIED to…most if not all of your life. So have I! It is a lie that has not only taken away our power but has held us emotional victims to life events and circumstances. The lie takes many forms, but the essence of the lie is *that external events are the source of all our emotional upsets.*

Our world seems to shout that you and I are NOT responsible for our emotional upset. Think about it. Wasn't it the "jerk" who pushed ahead of you at the ticket counter who really pissed you off? Or, isn't it that big test coming up that is making you a nervous wreck?

I once had a client, Carl (not his real name), who was

ordered by the court to come to counseling after having been arrested for breaking his neighbor's car window. Carl explained the situation as follows. "Doc, so I spent more than three hours shoveling snow outside of my house. This shit was heavy and icy. I cleaned a spot right in front of our house so that my wife would have a place to park. My neighbor, that SOB, came home from work and parked in the spot. I asked him nicely to move his car, and he just threw me the finger. Come on—wouldn't that piss you off?"

Well, what do you think? Wouldn't that piss you off?

Most people would answer yes to that question. After all, most people in our culture continue to delude themselves into thinking that life's events, pressures, and circumstance, even those carrying over from childhood, affect our moods, our emotional well-being. It is the traffic jam that makes me angry! It is the test grade that makes me upset and worried! It is the loss of a job—or opportunity—or even a loved one that makes me so depressed. We have been programmed to believe that it's not me, it is you or some event that is making me crazy and causing my emotional distress.

Now if all that sounds "correct," then you are a victim of the big lie.

The truth?

The truth is that no one can piss you off; nothing can make you a nervous wreck or make you feel guilty. That *responsibility*, as well as the *power to fix it*, rests within you.

Let's Face It—We Are All "Crazy" from Time to Time

I know that suggesting that you are crazy at times is probably not the best way to win your favor. I also recognize that using the word "crazy" is most likely not quite befitting my status as a professional psychologist. But in my defense, if we look at Webster's definition, we will find that "crazy" refers to a condition marked by thoughts and actions that lack reason. So fess up. Have you navigated all of life's moments with reason? I know that I haven't. There are times when I've "lost it."

I don't have to think hard to find a moment—or more than one moment—of my own craziness. Perhaps it was the time I stubbed my toe, only to curse the chair that "caused" it. Or maybe it was my squeezing of the steering wheel, with heart pounding, feeling anxiety while being stuck in a traffic jam and realizing that I was about to be late for an "important" meeting. Or, how about the time I was on the turnpike and approaching a toll booth when a driver on my left cut in front of me—nearly hitting the side of my car in the process. My reaction? Well, in addition to hitting my brakes, I blasted my horn and yelled expletives (in the confines of my car). I don't have a picture of how I must have looked, but I would imagine that I looked really "exercised" (that's a nice way of saying really pissed). Now, that entire car incident lasted only a few minutes, and happily, neither the driver of the other car nor I was harmed, but does any of this make my reaction rational?

If I accept the premise that rational responses help us adapt to the reality of a moment, I could argue that stepping on the brakes was a rational response. Would my prolonged honking of the horn, my yelling of obscenities, and what I assume was my elevated blood pressure and muscle tension be actions that were helping me adapt to the situation? Did these responses help me adjust and adapt to the situation, thus staying accident-free, or is it possible that these responses actually added to the discomfort and danger of the moment?

If my response (or at least part of it) neither reflected the reality of the moment nor helped me reach my goals (of safety) and adapt to the moment, then can we agree that at least for that moment I was not acting from reason and was, dare I say, being "crazy"?

Your Turn—Fess Up

Events like these happen every day. But the focus needs to be placed on the meaning we give to that event, not on the event itself. Quite often the meaning we assign actually distorts the importance of the event and as a result disrupts our emotional well-being.

Perhaps you experienced a time, such as being stuck in traffic or being unable to find your keys or phone, when you became frustrated and angry. In retrospect, does it now appear that your emotional reaction and behavioral responses were proportionate to the actual event? Did your emotional response at the time help you feel and act in ways that served you well? If your answer is no, then perhaps we can both agree that being "crazy," like being rational, is part of the human condition.

The good news?

Even if we accept that "crazy" is part of the human condition, we don't have to surrender to it. The key to defeating our crazies and achieving an emotionally healthy and well-balanced life is in understanding the role and function that our thinking, our meaning-making, our beliefs play in the creation of our emotions. Remember, contrary to the Big Lie, it is not people or circumstances outside of you that create your emotional reaction—*you* are doing that.

Defeating your crazies starts with understanding the connection between life events, our thoughts about those events, and the resulting emotions.

The A➔B➔C Connection

Conventional "wisdom" suggests that our emotions are consequences (C) of some activating event (A). From this position, I truly believe that it is the fact that the guy called me a name (A) that really made me mad (C). Contrary to this common "wisdom," external events are nothing more than experiences. They are experiences waiting to be given meaning. It is in this process of giving meaning to these events that we generate our own emotions.

Our emotions are NOT the direct response to the experience of an event. Instead, the sequence would be that there is some type of event or experience (**Activating event)** that we then interpret (**Belief)➔** and this interpretation or belief about the event results in the emotional experience **(Consequence).** This is the **A➔B➔C** of our emotional reactions.

Let's look at a straightforward illustration.

Have you ever been in a situation where someone was extremely fearful, even terrified, and you were not? I can remember taking a plane trip and sitting next to a young person, who, as the plane began to take off, showed signs of an anxiety attack. While we both experienced the physical effects of this takeoff (A, the activating event), our emotional responses (C) were different. As I looked about the cabin, it became clear that there was a variety of emotional responses being exhibited ranging from panic to glee. How can this be? How can the exact same event result in such different emotions? It all rested in the way each of us interpreted the event of taking off.

For those who on taking off had thoughts that led them to anticipate possible disaster, anxiety—even panic—resulted. Others appeared to have had their thoughts focused on the magazine article they were reading, or the work document on their computer, and they seemed almost unaffected (emotionally) by the event of takeoff. And for one child, who was looking out the windows and describing the clouds and the miniaturizing of the cars and houses on the ground, the experience appeared exhilarating, even joyful.

The same event and yet significantly different emotions

all as a function of how each individual interpreted or gave meaning to the event. This is the role and power of our thinking, our beliefs, in the creation of our emotions.

The following exercise may help to make this point clear.

The Power of Your Beliefs

Part I: Directions —In this part identify how you might feel if experiencing the event as described. There is a part II, but let's wait to explain that part.

Event/experience	Your feelings
(example) A person cuts ahead in the line boarding a plane.	Angry/annoyed/irritated
You got caught telling a lie.	
Your doctor called you to come in immediately to discuss your test results.	

A person calls you a derogatory name.	
A person with whom you have had a year-long relationship calls and abruptly ends that relationship without any explanation.	

Part II: Directions — Now, take another look at the situations, but this time identify what you would have to say to yourself, what you would have to believe about the event to generate the feeling(s) listed.

Event/experience	Self-talk/meaning given to the event	Generated feelings
(example) A person cuts ahead in the line boarding a plane.	I hope everything is okay. She looks likes she is in significant panic mode— perhaps she's missing her flight.	Concerned, curious

You got caught telling a lie.		Non-defensive and accepting responsibility
Your doctor called you to come in immediately to discuss your test results.		Relief
A person calls you a derogatory name.		Sadness for the individual
A person with whom you have had a year-long relationship calls and unexpectedly ends that relationship without any explanation.		Surprised but relieved

In reviewing this exercise were you able to change your feelings or the intensity of your feelings by assigning another meaning, another belief, another interpretation of the event? That is the power of our thinking in the creation of our emotions.

This ability to interpret or give meaning to our experiences can serve us well.

When our beliefs about an event are relatively accurate reflections of the actual event, then our emotional reactions, even when these are less than pleasant, will be both appropriate and useful for us at that moment. If, for example, you were walking down the street and were confronted by a huge, angry, snarling dog that was beginning to charge toward you, interpreting the situation as "potentially dangerous" would result in feelings of anxiety and bodily preparation for a fight-or-flight response. It could be argued that your interpretation reflected a real *possibility* of danger. Further, it would appear that the type of emotion (anxiety) resulting from this interpretation was useful in that it prepared you to defend yourself in the face of this possible danger. Your view of this situation appeared reasonable and useful—in other words, rational.

But how about the person who responds with that same level of anxiety in situations where there is little to no danger? Do you know someone who reacts with panic upon seeing a spider or garden snake? Perhaps you know someone who experiences extreme anxiety when faced with the responsibility of giving a speech or presentation? For these individuals the anxiety and the fear they experience, as well as their physical preparation for fight or flight, are real. And just as with the case of the individual responding to the charging dog, this anxiety, this reaction, is also the result of the individual's belief that these events (i.e., a spider, garden snake, or giving a speech) are threatening and dangerous. In this case, however, that interpretation of imminent danger is inaccurate. It is irrational. In this case, the belief in imminent danger is neither supported by the facts of the moment nor is that belief useful in helping them adapt or adjust to their reality. Just ask the "speech giver" who as a result of the high level of anxiety freezes at the podium and cannot remember a word of his prepared speech.

Interesting, But So What?

So maybe you are thinking, *Okay, so this interesting but...so what?* What is the value of this to you, to me?

Well, if the truth is that no one can piss me off—then that means I am the one causing my anger. If my anxiety is not the result of any event or circumstance, then that anxiety is the result of me "seeing" an event as dangerous. In other words, if my emotions and emotional reactions are self-generated, then the value of knowing this is that it empowers me to manage my reactions in a way that they not only support my emotional well-being but position me to adapt and respond to real-life situations effectively.

When we distort the actual events of our life, perhaps by assigning more importance or more negative conclusions than the event actually deserves, then the emotions aroused and actions taken often do anything but serve us well. These distorted beliefs are the *crazies* we need to recognize and learn to defeat.

Why Not Just Think Pleasant Thoughts?

Given that our emotions are the result of our view of life—the way we interpret our experiences—why not just go through life thinking only pleasant thoughts?

While such an approach to life may provide some short-term comfort, the truth is that emotions, including negative emotions, can help us adapt and effectively function in the face of life's challenges. Emotions—even those that are uncomfortable such as anxiety, anger, even guilt and shame—can serve us well. Our emotions can provide us with a quick, often highly adaptive way of responding to specific survival problems. Emotions provide us with powerful, physical messages that help us respond to our environment. Emotions, simply put, are or can be useful.

Look at each of the following situations and consider the potential value and usefulness of each of the emotions identified.

- Feeling anxious when confronted by a charging bull
- Feeling sad following the death of a loved one
- Being frustrated by the fact that the soda I selected is stuck in the machine

It could be argued that being anxious in the presence of a charging bull is useful if it initiates the person's flight response. The sadness experienced at the time of loss can invite reflections on all that the loved one meant and the special times shared. Even the frustration experienced with a stuck soda machine may motivate actions such as jiggling of the change return handle that results in the desired outcome. These feelings, even though unpleasant or uncomfortable, may have value in those specific circumstances.

It is important to recognize that emotions can be functional and serve us well. It is also important to note that emotions, our self-generated feelings, can at times be entirely dysfunctional and interfere with our adaptation and our happiness. Consider what happens in each of the previous situations when the events are interpreted in a way that not only distorts the truth of the moment but increases the level of emotion to a dysfunctional degree.

- Upon seeing the bulls (a block away), this person believes that they are doomed, and there is no way out. The anxiety experienced is so high that it freezes them in place or results in them passing out in the path of the charging bulls.
- The person experiencing a loss of a loved one now believes that he will no longer find joy in life. The sadness increases to the point where the grief is entirely overwhelming and interferes with the person's ability to function and challenges his desire to live.
- Or the person who is convinced, genuinely convinced, that everyone and everything is out to get him and as a result "sees" the stuck soda in the

machine as one more intolerable injustice. Perhaps the level of frustration and anger results not in a jiggle of the return money handle or a tap on the deposit shoot, but a foot through the front of the soda machine.

It would appear that for these individuals, their views of the situations not only fail to reflect the reality or facts of the moment but also fail to serve them in making the best out of this less-than-desirable situation.

To maintain our emotional well-being, we must be able to process information in a way that provides an accurate reflection of our reality at the moment. Interpreting things as they are will help us feel and act in ways that will serve us well.

But Sometimes Things Are Serious

Perhaps as you read the above, you may be saying something like, "Sure, I understand the concept, but there are real-life disasters and horrible events in life *that make people feel horrible.*"

Yes, there are times of serious life challenge, but even under these conditions, we remain the architect of our emotional reactions. Even in the midst of what may be termed a disaster, it is we who are making us feel horrible. Even under these conditions, we have the power to embrace these life events precisely as they are and attempt to adapt as best as possible OR we can reshape these events into horrible...unbearable...intolerable situations and experience emotional meltdown.

This point was vividly illustrated in the movie Titanic (Paramount Pictures and 20th Century Fox, 1997). In the movie, there is a scene in which the ship has its nose underwater, pitched eighty degrees and sinking rapidly. I think it is safe to suggest that most individuals would see this as an *undesirable event.*

In viewing that scene, I saw people who, given the circumstances, were very likely going to die within the next few minutes. But what caught my eye was how they responded to this event, this undesirable event.

Some of those about to die reacted in panic and jumped overboard, hastening their deaths. Others, with an outbreak of violence they probably rarely if ever displayed, pushed people aside and attempted to fight their way on to the lifeboats, even those that were also sinking. Yet within all of this chaos, there were others who seemed to make the best of an undesirable situation.

As the ship was sinking, with clear evidence that they had neither the time nor resources to save themselves, an elderly man and his wife lying in their stateroom chose to be together in a gentle, loving embrace during the time before their final gasp of air rather than using that time to respond in panic and horror. Similarly, musicians were standing on the deck who, upon realizing their lives were soon to end, picked up their instruments and used their final minutes of life to engage in something that they loved and enjoyed, playing their music.

Significantly different types of reactions to the same

life-ending event!

Since neither panic nor joy of holding a loved one would protect the individuals from their fate, the last moments of these people's lives were undoubtedly experienced differently (either painfully in panic; joyfully in shared love) as a result of how they processed the reality of this moment.

Understanding the role that your way of viewing or giving meaning to an event plays in the creation of your emotions opens the door to gaining control over those beliefs that result in dysfunctional feelings and behaviors. It opens the door to *defeating your crazies.*

Keep It Real: See It As It Is

The prescription for seeking and maintaining your emotional well-being is to engage in rational thinking. See things as they are—no better, no worse…just as they are.

Perhaps you know someone who employs the "ostrich" approach to life challenges. This is the "just bury your head and ignore unpleasant situations" approach. This is the person who upon seeing an unusual, dark, asymmetrical skin mole refuses the suggestion to see a doctor, stating and believing, "It's no big deal." While this viewpoint may provide short-term emotional relief, it is not an approach that will position that person to cope with the real demands of life, which in this case could be a real medical issue.

On the other hand, some people approach all of life's challenges with a "hair on fire" viewpoint. These individuals see things as worse than they are in reality. Processing the information from such a perspective not only intensifies the negative emotional experience of the situation but also often interferes with the person's ability to problem solve and adapt to the situation. This would be the case of a person who responds to the discovery of any skin discoloration as definitive evidence that they have melanoma and are surely going to die. Such an interpretation, without additional information, is a source of immediate pain and emotional upset and actually could block a useful behavior such as going to a doctor, since the belief may be "Why bother? I'm doomed."

In both of these situations, the individual is distorting the facts of the moment and in so doing fails to support their health and well-being. Your emotional health and well-being are best served when your thoughts and interpretations of life's events are neither rosy nor bleak but are an accurate reflection of reality.

Being Rational Ain't Easy

While the prescription is to see things as they are and learn to refuse to exaggerate or deflate their significance stubbornly, this prescription is not always easy to follow. One challenge is that we are often not aware that our beliefs—or the way we are making meaning—are distorting reality and causing us needless emotional upset. After all, we have become accustomed to our way of seeing our self and our world and making sense of it. It just seems natural.

A second challenge is that even when we become aware that the way we are creating meaning is less than rational and failing to serve our emotional health and well-being, we seem to be "wired" to defend it.

Perhaps you made reservations for an ocean cruise. Being excited, you share the news with a good friend. If in the process of sharing, your friend provides you with some information about the cruise line that challenges your decision to have invested so much money with them, you may find yourself either dismissing the importance of the data ("Oh yeah, I heard that, but that was just a few disgruntled travelers"), or providing counter information ("If I am not mistaken, that occurred under the old owner-ship; this is an entirely new group of management,") or even dismissing your friend ("Wow, couldn't you be a little happy that I am finally getting a vacation?"). Each of these responses is crafted to ensure that you could keep your original belief and excitement about choosing this cruise line and this particular vacation while coping with the new information.

Most of the times when we engage in such a defense of our beliefs, the results are relatively benign. There are times, however, when our inability to process all the data, especially those that do not support our way of thinking, results in upsetting negative emotions and unproductive behavior.

Consider the situation of a person experiencing de-pression. Often such an individual believes that things are utterly hopeless and that they are worthless (see chapter

9). When depressed a person often exaggerates all of his limitations or mistakes while at the same time minimizing evidence of his value. A friend who attempts to point out data which is disconfirming by saying something like: "Look, Fred, you have friends, a good job, and you are a super dad" may get a response such as: "Are you kidding? My friends are with me out of pity, and I'm way over my head at work. Who knows how long I can keep that job. Oh yeah...great dad, I haven't seen one of my daughter's basketball games in three weeks." The response is an attempt to reject the disconfirming information, thus allowing for the retention of the original belief about his personal worthlessness.

It can be safely stated that a person experiencing depression does not want to be depressed and does not want to hold on to depressive beliefs. But they, like we, are wired to defend their beliefs against attacks, even when those beliefs are ill-serving.

The Plan?

So what is the plan for attacking your ill-serving beliefs? The plan is for you to:

1. Understand and accept the power of your thinking, your beliefs, your interpretation of life's events as the source of your emotional experiences;

2. Become aware of the way you process information—the way you give meaning and see life's circumstances;

3. Identify those faulty ways that you process information, that is, identify your cognitive distortions;

4. Learn to challenge, debate, and replace distorted thoughts with rational thoughts; and

5. Eventually—modify your assumptions about yourself, others, and the world so that they support a more rational perspective on life.

If this seems like a difficult task, you are correct. The good news is that you have your entire lifetime to develop rational, functional thinking. Now, even though it is most likely that you will never *perfect* your ability to view life rationally, you will improve in that ability, and as a result, you will experience the benefits of such thinking in a very short time. The positive impact of embracing the principles and practice of cognitive therapy can be experienced quickly, but for those results to endure, we will need to practice...practice...practice.

So, let's begin.

CHAPTER **2**

Recognizing and Owning Our "Crazies"

If a problem is fixable, if a situation is such that you can do something about it, then there is no need to worry. If it's not fixable, then there is no help in worrying.

Dalai Lama

THE QUOTE FROM the Dalai Lama appears to make sense. It certainly seems rational. Too bad that it is not something that most of us embrace or employ when confronted with life's challenges. For many of us, worrying about things over which we have no control is almost a daily pastime. And for some of us, worrying at levels that block our ability to fix the issue at hand is all too common.

Humans are uniquely rational...at times. When you and I process our experiences in ways that genuinely reflect the facts of the moments, it positions us to feel and act in ways that serve as well. It would be nice, and this would be a short book if this were always the case.

The truth is that we have abundant examples in our day-to-day interactions that highlight the fact that humans are not always rational. You and I often process our experiences in ways that not only distort the facts of the moment but as a result set us up for the "crazies" (i.e., emotional conditions which are neither desirable nor useful). Learning to recognize these distortions, challenge them, and replace them with more rational thoughts is truly our key to defeating these "crazies."

Even Minor "Craziness" Is a Waste

The uselessness of our distorted thinking is not restricted to those times of major life crises or to those individuals identified as exhibiting a clinical syndrome. As you navigate your day, you will have ample opportunity to respond to one of life's "minor" challenges with crazy thinking and dysfunctional reactions.

Take a moment to consider those little life challenges that often greet your day. Perhaps it is walking out of your house to find your car with a flat tire, or maybe it is the discovery of an overdue bill or a rip in your favorite sweater or even that moment when your pencil point breaks. These are not exceptional events, and some could argue these are not even things worth considering, but each of these experiences invites our emotional and behavioral response. For some the response, even if it is just for a moment, increases the discomfort of that moment and interferes with effective adjustment to these challenges. Cursing upon seeing the flat tire or tossing the broken pencil would not qualify as pathological, but they certainly are not useful in making the best of these moments.

I, for one, want my responses to the challenges and inconveniences of life to be as life-giving and adaptive as reality will allow. To do this, I will need to recognize how I am misinterpreting and distorting the facts of the moment and reformulate that thinking so that it is much more rational and functional. One of the strategies that can help us develop a process of recognizing the level of rationality or functionality to our thinking, and adjusting as needed, is to keep a thought journal.

Journaling: Helping with Perspective

Let's imagine that your friend comes to you, clearly very upset, in absolute panic mode and despair. She explains that she made what she called a significant error at work and is sure she is going to lose her job. "That's it! I know I'm going to be fired." As she shares her story, it becomes clear to you that she is focusing, almost exclusively, on this one mistake. Given what you know about your friend and some of the other details that she has shared about her work and work performance, you find it unlikely that this one mistake would be cause for her dismissal. As she continues, she says things such as: "I am just a loser,"

"I should never have been given that promotion," and "I am not sure I should be in this field." As you listen you find yourself almost automatically recalling information that is in clear contrast to her statements.

For example, you remember that she has been promoted (multiple times), which to you is evidence of her value and competence. You remember her telling you about the project she is managing and how difficult it is and how everyone has been amazed that it has gone so smoothly. You remember her telling you that a couple of months back, a colleague made a similar mistake with no serious consequences. As you consider all of these pieces of information, you find yourself "debating" with her about the likelihood of her being fired. It is not as if you are merely trying to comfort her; you genuinely see the event and the assumed consequences differently.

The fact that your friend was singularly focused on this one mistake—ignoring other data, other information—resulted in her extreme despair. While her upset is real, it appears to be the result of her failing to engage all of the information relevant to the event before drawing her conclusion. If only she could see the event as you did. If only she could stop and process all of the information, all the facts of her work experience, before drawing a conclusion regarding her job status. If she did, it is likely that the intensity of her upset would be diminished. If only she could approach this situation more rationally. Yes, if only.

The process of journaling is one in which you write down a description of the event associated with your emotional upset, describe your feelings, and then most importantly list your thoughts, your beliefs, or the meaning that you gave to that event.

Using the example of our "friend," as the reference, the journal may look something like this.

Event: "I turned in the report and forgot to add the latest financial projections."

Feelings: "I am horrified. I feel in panic mode."

Thoughts: "Oh my God, the data I included are not accurate. I am so friggin dumb. How could I do this? This is unbelievable, I'm toast. There is no way they are not going to freak out and make an example of me. What the hell am I going to do? I need this job—and if it gets out, I'll never work in this field again."

The value of such journaling is that it provides you with the opportunity to review an event associated with the time of your upset, while at the same time inviting you to consider all the data, all of the relevant facts that may or may not support your interpretations. It is in critically reviewing the validity of your initial interpretation that you may come to realize that you were engaging in distorted, less-than-rational thinking (i.e., the "crazies").

So as our "friend" reviews her thoughts about the incident, she may find thoughts emerging that are not supportive of her initial interpretations. Thus, she may begin to note:

"Wait, only the last quarter of data was missing, and

those data were very similar to the previous three quarters. It needs to be included in the report, but it really doesn't change the conclusions."

"Roman (the president/CEO) never freaks out—nor is it his style to humiliate anyone publicly. His style is to talk to you privately, and the only time it's a problem is when you don't know what went wrong and how to avoid it recurring. I know what went on, and what to do."

"This is serious, but not a disaster. I can resubmit... no...I will resubmit an adjusted report adding the new data."

It is this process of debating the original thoughts about the situation by including all of the relevant data that your thoughts, your beliefs about the event will be reformulated to be more objective, more rational. Such a reformulation will result in an adjustment to your emotional reaction. So for our friend who was initially in panic and despair—the new perspective will help her feel concerned, somewhat anxious, and motivated to make the needed corrections.

This process of journaling can be particularly useful in situations where the upset continues past the initial event or when you find yourself stuck in rehashing the particulars of a time of upset. Revisiting that event or experience will help you reframe the meaning in such a way as to allow you to move on. In addition, the practice of journaling will help you develop the habit of: (a) "hearing" your thoughts and your beliefs about events; (b) challenging those that are less than rational, and (c) reformulating your interpretation of an event so that it is more rational and functional, thus contributing to your emotional well-being. With practice, this process will become almost automatic, reducing, if not eliminating, your "crazies" and resulting in a healthier and happier approach to life and all its challenges.

How to Start

There is no one right way or single format or style to employ while journaling. Whether you maintain an ongoing narrative or use a more structured approach, such as the six-column method illustrated at the end of this chapter, the journal should include each of the following.

STEP 1: THE FEELINGS

It is likely that the first thing that has your attention as you begin journaling is the way you are feeling. So you can start by identifying the emotions, the feelings that are the focus of the journal entry. Describe your feelings and perhaps even grade the intensity using your own scale. So, for example, you may list something like, "Stressed, 80%; Angry 60%."

STEP 2: THE EVENT OR EXPERIENCE

The second step in journaling is to write out a description of the event. This event could be recent or even a historical event that you remember at this moment. So, for example, let's assume I am upset about being given a work assignment at the end of my workday. I might write: "It is 3:30, on Friday and my boss just gave me three more reports to complete by 5 p.m., today."

It is essential to approach this task as objectively as possible. Just the facts, or at least the facts as you remember them.

Now, these first two steps are relatively easy to do; the next one may pose a bit of a challenge.

STEP 3: IDENTIFY YOUR THOUGHTS ABOUT THE EVENT

Now that you have identified the details of the situation, it is important to review those details and, as you do, attempt to tune into your thoughts about the situation. What is your self-talk? What are your thoughts that seem to be evaluating the event? What meaning are you giving to this event?

Identifying your evaluative thoughts can be quite a challenging thing, especially since your thoughts can happen at various levels of awareness, and those serving as the source of your emotional reactions may not be immediately apparent.

Much of what and how we are thinking is quite apparent to us at any one moment. Just stop for a moment and "listen." What thoughts are you having? Are you thinking about this book, or what you need to do next, or about something happening around you? While these thoughts are clear and obvious, we also have the ability to generate thoughts that are not as immediately apparent. Many of our thoughts, our ways of processing events and experiences, have been employed so frequently that they have become habitual. These thoughts may operate below our immediate level of awareness. Since these thoughts are often the source of our upset, it is important to pay special attention to their presence. To illustrate the nature of these somewhat "automatic" thoughts, consider the following little thought experiment.

Imagine that you were walking down the street and found yourself confronted by a person holding a gun, stating, "Stick them up." It may be safe to assume that you would experience anxiety at that moment. The question is why?

If we could turn up the volume of your self-talk at the moment, we would very likely hear you identify and give meaning to the situation with thoughts such as: *That's a gun. He's robbing me.* You are aware of these thoughts, and they appear to be an accurate identification of what is occurring. But are these thoughts the source of your anxiety? No.

In this case, the anxiety you were feeling was not a direct result of your thought *that's a gun*, but rather that additional thought, which may have been almost unconsciously linked to these first thoughts and went like this: *That's a gun...oh my god, I'm going to die!* It is this second thought, one predicting immediate and extreme danger, that serves as the source of your anxiety.

This second level of interpretation often occurs so

rapidly and almost without full awareness that the thoughts can go unchallenged and accepted as true, without evaluating their validity. This is usually not a problem. But it can be problematic if the automatic thoughts directing our responses are distorting reality, resulting in feelings and behaviors that are disruptive to our well-being, and interfering with our adaptive functioning.

So as you attempt to identify your interpretation of the specific event about which you are journaling, keep pushing yourself to write out the thoughts going through your head. Ask yourself questions such as: "What does the event mean to me?" "What do I think will happen?" "What does this imply or suggest about others?" "What does it suggest about me?" It is important to push yourself to keep asking and answering the question "So what?"

If I return to my own illustration of the late afternoon work assignment, I may find that now I write down an immediate thought, something like: "That is a lot of work she just gave me." If I challenge myself to go deeper in an attempt to see if other, more automatic thoughts were involved, I would ask, "So what? So what does that mean?" In posing such a question, I might find that I was also thinking: "So what? So I can't believe she is asking me to do all of this stuff. It's always me. I never get a break. She always takes advantage of me. It is so unfair!"

Now, an interpretation such as this, while possible but yet to be proven, could result in feelings beyond the initial stress tied to the increased workload. Believing *this is unjust* and *she is always out to get me* could serve as the source for my elevated stress and anger. The question to consider would be "Is this interpretation, this meaning-making, valid and an accurate view of reality?" If not, then there is a chance that my reaction is ill-placed and not useful.

A caution is in order. Because you and I are fundamentally rational, it is possible that when you start writing your thoughts down and re-reading what you are writing, you may begin to feel that the thoughts, viewed now in print, are silly. And you may want to either not continue to write them down or dismiss them. DON'T.

Yes, they may seem silly now, but they didn't at the time of the upset. These thoughts may appear stupid now because you are viewing them from a different perspective. These might be the very thoughts or patterns of thinking that we need to reformulate.

STEP 4: IDENTIFYING OUR "CRAZIES" (THOUGHTS THAT ARE IRRATIONAL)

As you review your interpretations of the events that you listed, you may begin to see that the meaning you gave to that event failed to be an accurate, objective interpretation. I know that I can point to times where I have interpreted a relatively normal experience such as being caught in a traffic jam as having more importance, more significance than it deserved. At this step, you should review the meaning that you assigned to the event and begin to assess the degree to which it is an accurate, objective, and rational reflection of that event. It is important to identify any and all of the facts that support your original belief while at the same time being open to any evidence that fails to support that interpretation. Looking at my belief that "this always happens to me" (about being stuck in traffic), I am quick to see that this is not true, that it may frequently happen, especially at this time of day, but not always. It is in challenging ourselves to identify, as best as possible, the truth of the event that we will be able to reformulate our belief so that it supports a healthier and more functional emotional and behavioral response.

The fact that we sometimes distort the meaning of an event—bend the truth of the moment—is to be expected. As I noted in chapter 1, as a human, you (and I) can be both rational and irrational. Cognitive therapists like Aaron Beck and David Burns have been able to identify patterns of faulty and dysfunctional thinking. An abbreviated listing of the more common forms of these cognitive errors is presented in the table listed below. There is a very good chance that as you read the description of these errors, you will discover that you have employed many of these in your own interpreting of life events. I know I have.

We will discuss these in greater detail in the chapters that follow, as they contribute to particular forms of emotional upset such as stress, anxiety, anger, guilt, shame, and depression. For now, it is important for you to learn to be aware of times when you are engaging in such cognitive errors so that you can challenge and replace this faulty thinking with more rational, useful thoughts.

A Sampling of Distorted Information Processing (Cognitive Errors)

All-or-Nothing Thinking: A person engaging in this type of thinking sees things as only black or white. Events—other's actions or even your own—are viewed as extremes: you are either perfect or a total failure. This would be the case of the person determined to lose weight, and who following one slip off her diet decides, "What the hell, that diet is blown, so I might as well order a second dessert." For a person engaged in all-or-none thinking, there is no other way to see an event; there is no in-between.

Overgeneralization: In this case, a person takes a single negative event and concludes that all similar situations will be the same. For example, assume that I invite a person on a date, and I am rejected. If I conclude that all people I ask will deny me, then I am employing an overgeneralization. Or, perhaps you had a bad experience with one dog. If you now assume all dogs will be a danger to you, you are engaging in overgeneralization. The use of (and belief in) words such as "always" and "never" may provide a clear indication that overgeneralization is being engaged to find meaning at that moment.

Mental Filters/Selective Abstraction: When using this form of dysfunctional thinking, a person pulls out only the bad events in their lives and overlooks the positives. It is like we have a filter that allows some information in (negative details) and excludes any contradictory positive information. The result is that the person's view of all reality becomes tainted by that negativity.

For example, imagine that a person just received a printed assessment of their job performance. Assume that the actual evaluation contained seven areas identified as highly proficient and one area that was identified as needing improvement. If the individual began to obsess about the one area needing improvement, even to the point of concluding that they were messing up at their job—they would be employing selective abstraction.

Jumping to Conclusions: As suggested by the title, this error in information processing occurs when a person draws a grand conclusion based solely on insufficient information. For example, if you are trying to contact an elderly relative and the phone rings and rings and rings with no answer and as a result you conclude that your relative has fallen or has died, this would be jumping to conclusions. Similarly, if you walk into work and see a message stating that your boss wants to speak with you and you immediately become anxious "knowing" that you are going to be fired, then again, you are engaging in this form of cognitive error.

Magnification (Catastrophizing)/Minimization:
With this form of cognitive error, a person exaggerates the significance of an event or piece of information. The bullied teen who believes the embarrassment is utterly unbearable and that she can't go on would be engaging in this type of cognitive distortion. Yes—things are difficult and not as desired—but are they factually unbearable?

The other side of this distortion is the process of reducing or minimizing the importance of some experience or event. This would be the case for the person who chooses to ignore some medical symptom and refuses to have it checked out, stating: "It's no big deal!"

Emotional Reasoning: Emotional reasoning occurs when a person uses their emotions, their feelings, as the basis for drawing conclusions about reality. The thinking is…"If I feel it, it must be true."

This would be the case of a person who is experiencing anxiety, concluding that there must be something dangerous about to happen. "I am terrified of taking off on this plane. I know it's going to crash." Or, a person who is feeling overwhelmed with a work assignment and uses this feeling as the basis for concluding that it is hopeless and that the job can't be done.

Shoulds and Musts: Those who engage in this form of information processing firmly believe that they and the world should be a certain way, a way that they define as necessary. When applied to oneself, "should" often results in guilt and frustration. "I can't believe I got that question wrong—I should know better." When we employ "shoulds" and "musts" when viewing the actions of others, we often experience increased frustration and anger, since it is likely they are not adhering to our "rules." With "should" and "must" beliefs, we take something that we would wish would be or merely desire and turn it into a mandate, a "have to." Comments such as: "They have no right saying that!" Or, "How dare they act like that?" reflect an individual's self-created rules for the world, rules that they feel are being violated.

STEP 5: DEBATE AND REFORMULATE

As you review your interpretation of the event connected to your upset, you hopefully will gain a more complete and accurate picture of the event. With this new perspective, you will be able to reformulate the meaning you have assigned to the event so that it more accurately reflects the reality of that moment.

In challenging your original thinking about the event, ask yourself the following questions and use your response to the questions to reshape your initial thoughts. The goal is to create a belief that accurately reflects the facts of the moment.

- Is this interpretation accurate? True? Does it reflect the facts of the moment, actual reality? If not, what would be true?
- Am I jumping to conclusions? If I saw my thoughts as hypotheses rather than facts, would the evidence completely support them? Part of them?
- Am I exaggerating or overemphasizing a negative aspect of the situation? What other less negative or even positive elements have I filtered out?
- Am I catastrophizing? (*Am I making it seem worse than it is?*) What is the most reasonable and realistic worst-case scenario?
- How do I know it will happen? (*Am I a mind reader?*) Where's the evidence?
- Is there another way to look at the situation?
- If my friend were thinking this way, how would I argue with them?

Each of the questions posed is intended to help you reconsider the "facts" of the events so that you can adjust the interpretation to more accurately reflect those facts. So if we return to my example of the late afternoon work assignment, and my initial interpretation of it was "unfair," "always me," and that I was being "taken advantage of," I quickly see that these are inaccurate distortions of reality.

- Yes, it is close to the end of my workday, and the boss did just give me three reports to complete. However, she also asked Allison to do a couple, so I guess it is NOT always me. (*Filtering/Selective Abstraction error*)
- She did "apologize" for the late assignment. She sounded sincere. Maybe she is not trying to take advantage of me. (*Filtering/Selective Abstraction error*)
- The reports only need final editing, and that takes ten to fifteen minutes each. So why am I catastrophizing this? It is part of my job and can most likely be completed in my normal workday hours. (*Catastrophizing/Maximizing error*)
- She has allowed me to leave early on a couple of days so that I could see my son's baseball game, so she doesn't always mistreat me. (*Selective Abstraction/Filtering Error*)
- She has the right to ask me to do this work—it is my job, so sitting here getting angry is not helping get the reports done or me out the door; it is just upsetting me. (*Should/Must error*)

Reviewing my initial view of the assignment with these new data will change my interpretation of the event in such a way that I may still feel disappointed, having hoped to get out early, but not angry or down because of my incorrect belief that this was unfair and I was being abused. Such a reformulation of the meaning given to this event is not only more factually based, but it is also much more functional in that I am no longer wasting energy, nor emotional capital by making myself angry. I am now able to focus and efficiently complete the reports so that I can be on my way.

As you review your own initial interpretations of the event and attempt to respond to the questions that challenge that interpretation, allow your reflections to guide the reformulation of your interpretation of the event.

Should you debate and reformulate your thoughts about an event that has long passed? Your rethinking is not going to change the event or your initial reaction to it, but the process is undoubtedly useful at those times when you find yourself reliving the event and the upset. But beyond this value, the benefit of this process is that it is training you in a way of interpreting life events that is more reality-based, less distorted and dysfunctional, and, if you will allow me...less "crazy."

With practice, this new way of approaching life challenges will become almost automatic, and you will find that it not only contributes to your successful adjustment at that moment but also to your overall emotional well-being.

One Form of Journaling (An Illustration)

As stated there is no "right" way to keep your journal as long as it helps you identify and reformulate faulty information processing. One format often employed is a table such as that illustrated below. The example used is of a graduate student who is attempting to respond more rationally and functionally to receiving a failing grade. A blank form of this table is provided for your use. You may find it helpful to not only engage in the six-column process, but begin to identify any recurrent patterns of cognitive distortion. The more you become aware of these, the easier it will be to debate and reformulate.

An Illustration of Thought Journaling

DESCRIBE EVENT:

I received an F on my paper with numerous negative comments.

MEANING ASSIGNED SELF-TALK

Oh my god. I'm going to fail this course. This is horrible. I'll flunk out of the program. How am I ever going to face my family? I'm such a loser.

FEELINGS/ BEHAVIOR

Panic, feelings of depression and shame (emotions), deciding just to quit going to class (behavior)

POINTS OF DEBATE

Wait. Aren't there multiple grades in this class? How is failing one paper evidence I will fail the course? Also, does the program policy allow for retaking courses?

And how about the policies of retention in the program? Does failing one course mean that I am out of the program?

So the worst case is I fail out of the program. I know my family loves me; how would failing the program change or remove that love?

New thought

This is concerning, and confusing. I've done well on other papers. I wonder where I went wrong here. I need to discuss this with my professor. Also, I should check the policy regarding redoing assignments and how one lousy grade reflects on my continued status in the program.

New feelings and behaviors

Concerned,

confused,

committed

to meet with the professor

My Journal

Date:_____

Cognitive Distortions Identified:

_____

DESCRIBE EVENT:

_____

_____

_____

_____

MEANING ASSIGNED SELF-TALK

_____

_____

_____

_____

_____

FEELINGS/ BEHAVIOR

_____

_____

_____

_____

_____

POINTS OF DEBATE

_____

_____

_____

_____

_____

NEW THOUGHT

_____

_____

_____

_____

NEW FEELINGS AND BEHAVIORS

_____

_____

_____

_____

_____

SECTION II:
THE DOWNSIDE TO DISTORTED
THINKING (AKA OUR CRAZIES)

CHAPTER 3

Stressing About Stress

WHICH OF THE following do you think may be a cause for stress?

- Your car skidding on an icy road
- Being handed a significant work (or school) assignment that is due within the next day
- Getting divorced
- Getting married
- Winning the lottery

Well, if you identified each of the above as a potential cause for stress, you would be correct. While most often we recognize events that are negative as stressful, or perhaps more accurately *distressful*, the truth is that positive experience can also be stressful, which in this case we label as *eustress*.

The term "stress" was coined by Hans Selye, a

Hungarian-born endocrinologist, in 1936. Selye defined stress as: "the non-specific response of the body to *any demand for change"(italics added)*. If you re-read that definition, you may be struck, as was I, by the reference of stress as a response to ANY demand for change. Any!

That would suggest that sliding on a slippery road or falling off a skateboard, both of which demand adaptation, would be stressful. It also means that adjusting to marriage, divorce, sickness, getting a new job, even digesting a particularly spicy meal could be stressful, assuming that they require some form of adaption or change. So it is clear that stress is part of the human condition and thus cannot be, nor should be, eliminated. It can, however, be managed.

The Stress Response

Selye (1907–1982) hypothesized that the body goes through a process he termed the **General Adaptation Syndrome (GAS). He noted that this process has three stages:** alarm, resistance, and exhaustion. Despite its imprecision, the GAS has proven to be a useful model for understanding our response to stress as well as instructive on steps to facilitate adaption and reduce the adverse effects of prolonged stress.

ALARM STAGE

The alarm reaction stage refers to the initial changes the body undergoes when stressed. Consider the situation in which you are driving your car and hit an icy patch on

47

the road or hydroplane on a wet spot. As you feel the car start skidding, you may become aware that your heart rate is increasing, your respiration is elevated, and you are feeling a bit of an adrenaline rush. These are all manifestations of the "alarm" state, in which your body is attempting to maximize your preparation for coping with this potentially dangerous situation.

With this adrenaline rush, you will find that not only have you been aroused from your road-coma but are now in a state of rapid, almost automatic responding, all aimed at correcting the sliding car and returning to a safe and stable drive. These initial reactions certainly can prove helpful in making the adaptions necessary for the maintenance of our well-being. The problem occurs when this level of response is prolonged, or when the intensity of the response is disproportional and thus ineffective in helping us adapt to a stressor.

RESISTANCE STAGE

Staying at a maxed-out state of arousal is neither sustainable nor genuinely adaptive, so we attempt to lower our response to an appropriate level given the specific nature of the stress demand. As such, after the initial shock of a stressful event and engaging in an alarm response, we begin to adjust (lower) the amount of stress hormone (cortisol) being secreted, and our heart rate, blood pressure, and respiration move to a more normalized level.

The degree of preparedness that we experience in this

resistance change should be at a level that helps us to adapt or adjust to the demand as quickly and effectively as possible and with the least amount of energy expenditure. Thus, upon feeling the skid, you fight the tendency to jam on the brakes and exert maximum force on the steering wheel, moving toward a more controlled response—one that will prove more effective in the situation.

While the physical response to stress is generally toned down during a resistance stage, remaining in this stage for an extended period can lead to exhaustion.

Exhaustion Stage

Struggling with stress for long periods of time can drain your physical, emotional, and mental resources to the point where your body no longer has the strength to fight stressors. You may give up or feel your situation is hopeless. The physical effects of this stage can also weaken your immune system and put you at risk for a variety of stress-related illnesses.

Thinking and Its Contribution to Your Stress

While it is clear that you cannot eliminate stress given the ever-present demands for change and adaptation you encounter each day, there are clearly things that can be done to help you avoid the exhaustion stage and move through resistance as effectively and efficiently as possible. To do so, you need to understand the role of your cognition—your thinking—in the creation and mainte-nance of prolonged stress.

Imagine a situation in which you were driving on a highway and as you navigated around a bend, you found yourself in the direct line of an oncoming truck. Given the danger presented you most likely would experience the alarm stage and with that react almost unconsciously, slamming on the brakes and swerving out of the way. The alarm state, while anything but comfortable, also helped to employ rapid response resources and remove you from the source of the danger.

Following this encounter, you may find it difficult to re-turn to your pre-event level of stress, even after the danger has passed. You may notice that your heart remains beating rapidly, your respiration is still quick and shallow, and your hold on the steering wheel now resembles a white-knuck-led death grip, even though you are well past the location of the "almost-accident." Why? Why so stressed? The real danger has passed, and you adapted successfully. What is the source of this prolonged stress?

We begin to get a hint about what is happening if we think about what is entailed in the resistance stage. In or-der for us to turn down our stress response from the all-out alarm state to a more measured response, one matching the actual demands of the stressor, we need to interpret the events that are occurring, at the moment, and identify the level and forms of adaption required. Stress is genuinely a participating event in that it involves a stimulating event but also our interpretation of that event. It is the meaning that we give to the event that produces the level of resistance employed.

So if you remained at a high level of stress response even though you were now well past the ongoing truck, it might be that even though the situation changed, your interpretation may not have. The facts are that the truck has passed and the accident was avoided. The facts are that you are now riding safely back on track to your destination. But if you remained at a high level of stress response, it is likely that your focus was not on the facts of your current situation, but instead you were rehashing (and thus reliving) the incident. It is also possible that your current stress level was further elevated by immersing yourself in thinking about "what-could-have-been." These self-generated thoughts distort the reality of our moment and are the source of the very high and prolonged experience of stress.

It is undoubtedly true that environmental conditions or physical events can present us with a demand to adapt and as a result serve as sources of stress. From the demands encountered during times of war, or natural disaster, to the less dramatic conditions of stress experienced while moving from a chilly room to one that is hot, it is clear that physical events serve as a source for much of the stress we encounter. It is also true that our stress experience and stress response are impacted by the way we give meaning to these conditions.

Regardless of the actual situation, the way we give meaning to the event and our perception of its impact on us will determine the amount of stress we experience. When our appraisal of the situation is a distortion of the reality, attributing more danger to it than is deserved, our stress will be disproportionate to the actual demands faced.

The role of our thoughts in the creation and maintenance of stress is apparent when contrasting the way two different individuals react to the same situation. Consider the following illustration. Two people sit in the waiting area of a local diagnostic testing center. Both are scheduled to undergo a magnetic resonance imaging (MRI) scan. An MRI is a standard procedure used by hospitals and employs a strong magnetic field and radio waves to create detailed images of the organs and tissues within the body. It is a non-invasive and non-painful procedure. It does, however, require an individual to lie flat for a period of time, moving through a tube-shaped scanner. The scanner, which varies in diameter from fifty-five to seventy centimeters, is, for the average adult, tight.

So we have two people, the same test and same scanner, and wildly different stress levels. While one waits for the scheduled test by sitting back in the chair and reading the magazines provided, the other shows clear signs of increased stress. The second person appears to be having trouble relaxing. He is pacing throughout the waiting area, going back and forth to the desk nurse to check in on the starting time for his test. He is sweating, and his complexion is flushed. Here is a situation where the actual event is the same for both individuals, yet there are dramatically different stress responses.

Given the active and significant contribution that our

own thinking and interpretation of life events have to the experience of our stress, it becomes clear that learning to control our thoughts so that they accurately reflect the situation as it is—no better, no worse—will help us manage our stress responses.

Our Stress-Inducing "Crazies" (aka Distorted Thoughts)

So a quick test. Have you ever felt and actually believed that there was something you truly couldn't stand? I am not talking about a moment of merely using a word or a phrase that you know was exaggerating the intensity of a moment. I am asking you to consider a time when you honestly felt and believed that the situation was one that you could no longer endure.

If you ever found a time in your life when the demands or the conditions you were experiencing were such that you genuinely felt as if they were unbearable, that you could no longer stand it, take a moment now and ask yourself: Was that true? I mean...didn't you in fact "stand it," "bear it"?

Now, I am not suggesting we minimize the many serious challenges experienced in life. What I am suggesting, however, is that when presented with significant challenges to our survival, it is essential that we don't contribute to their stress-effect by adding an inaccurate and more devastating interpretation of the situation than the reality would support. Believing something is unbearable, genuinely believing that you can't stand it, maximizes the danger and stress of that situation.

It is important to realize that at this point in your life, you have not encountered something that was unbearable. You have most likely experienced things that were difficult to endure or even survive, but if you are reading this—you did.

Sadly when we buy into the perspective that what we are encountering is unbearable, we are distorting reality and, as a result, creating an exaggerated and disproportionate level of stress. In order for you to manage stress in a way that will help you effectively adjust to life demands while maintaining your emotional well-being, you will need to learn to identify those times when you are distorting the situation and then develop the ability to challenge and reformulate those distorted thoughts in order to more accurately adjust to the reality of the moment.

The following are some cognitive errors or distortions that can contribute to the creation and maintenance of dysfunctional levels of stress.

PERFECTIONISM: NEEDING TO BE THE PERFECT "ME"

Just imagine if the test you were about to take or the speech you were just starting to deliver were actually singular measures of your total worth as a human being. If you fail—you are a failure. Anything less than perfect will result in the general rejection by all as evidence that you are a loser.

Now I know that is dramatic, but for some who hold a belief that they need to be "perfect," such a perspective is exactly what they bring to typical life-challenges. For those with a need to be perfect, tasks such as presenting in front of a group, going for a job interview, participating in a meeting, or even engaging in a social gathering can illicit debilitating stress. After all, from their perspective, these are not merely normal social activities but, in their way of thinking, tests of their total self-worth. Now that is stressful. Believing that you must be thoroughly competent in all things to be worthwhile and acceptable will clearly elevate normal life stressors to a "life-and-death" status.

The "prescription" for anyone rigidly holding on to such perfectionistic thinking is to learn to accept the fact that human beings, by very definition, are less than perfect. One will make mistakes, and making a mistake or even multiple mistakes is not evidence that one is worthless, rather, just a fallible human being.

While mistakes are clearly not something one seeks, they are something that we all encounter. If you are a person who engages in such perfectionistic thinking, consider the following: Do you feel that all those you love, who by definition of being human make mistakes, are worthless and unacceptable as a result of those mistakes? If you don't hold the same perfectionistic standard for all, then how arbitrary and irrational is it to apply it to only yourself? Are you that special?

To help remind you of your less-than-perfect human

nature, you may want to write out the following reflection, post it, and review it daily. The message?

Making a mistake or even multiple errors may be undesirable, but it does not make me worthless. Mistakes are evidence that I am fallible and merely human.

In addition to accepting your fallibility as a human, you can defeat the craziness of perfectionistic thinking by employing each of the following:

1. Reality Check on Goals: Make sure the goals you seek are reasonable and reachable.

2. Embrace Mistakes: Rather than hiding, denying, or decrying your mistakes, embrace them. It's okay if others see you mess up. Just remind yourself that an error can be an opportunity for growth. Embrace it, review it, analyze it, and look at what you can learn from it. The one thing we know you can learn is that you are not perfect, and that is perfectly normal and acceptable.

3. Challenge What It Means: Okay, so you got 100 percent on that test, beat everyone at the golf outing, and you even have the "ideal" body fat percentage...so what? What does any of this really mean? Which on the list of achievements makes you a better human being, the best human being? What on the list will matter in one day or twenty years? Enjoy but keep perspective on what it all really means about you. You are the same person you were before the achievement, and that was

and remains good enough.

4. Celebrate You: Strive to be the best reflection of you, accepting, even celebrating your quirks, wrinkles, and idiosyncrasies.

THE WORLD ACCORDING TO ME (MY SHOULDS AND MUSTS):

Do you know someone who gets hugely stressed when there is a traffic jam or the waiter is running a bit slow with his order—or even when the soda in the vending machine gets stuck? Okay, we can agree that these situations are less than desirable. It is also true that each of these events elicits stress by the fact that they require us to make some form of adaptation. But for some people, the stress levels experienced appear disproportionate to the event and can result in anything but adaptive responding. I mean really, does the slow traffic require such an onslaught of curse words and horn blowing, or the soda machine a foot to its front? If you know someone like this, then there is a good chance that she engages in the cognitive error of "shoulding" and "musting."

One of the "crazies" (i.e., cognitive distortions) that can contribute to our stress is the belief that the world and those in it should be a certain way, a way that we define as acceptable. Rigidly believing that the "waiter *should* be here," or there "*should not* be any traffic at this time," or that person "*has no right* to be or act that way" are all examples of such distortions.

Operating from a belief system that the world (and others) should act and be as you define sets you up to be extremely stressed, annoyed, even angry when the world and others are not operating as they SHOULD. Now, that may seem a bit extreme. But we have evidence of the severe reactions that can result from such rigid beliefs. Just consider the all-too-many examples of road rage that ended in acts of violence. Quite often this behavior was a response to an event such as having another car cut in front at a toll booth or a driver failing to immediately move when a traffic light turns green. Think about it—extreme stress, violent behavior in the face of what objectively could be called minor situations. But apparently for these individuals, the events were not interpreted as minor—they were seen as significant violations of their "Shoulds."

Yes, these are extreme examples, and they hopefully are not something that you have experienced. But even beyond these extremes, the damage of "shoulding" can be seen in less dramatic forms throughout your day. Just consider those little events in life that may not go the way you would have preferred. Perhaps you experienced a time when your shoelace snapped, or someone beat you to the parking spot you were eyeing, or you discovered that someone failed to follow through on a commitment they made. If you found that you responded with a heightened level of stress and annoyance, it is likely that you processed these events through a belief that these were unfair and some violation of a rule or mandate. It is a belief that none of these things would be happening if you made up the rules for the world and the world did what it should. While we may desire to make things the way we wish, or the way we would prefer, holding rigidly to the belief that people or events SHOULD be the way we want creates undue stress.

If you are a person who is locked into SHOULDS, it is crucial to remind yourself that it would be interesting (not necessarily desirable, just interesting) IF you possessed the power to make up the rules for the world. However, you do not, and it is much more efficient, much less stressful to embrace the moment as it is, even while you consider ways of making it better for yourself. Yes, that parking space has been taken, but does the heightened stress make your moment better or provide a space? The shoelace snapped; does the stress help you decide on an alternative?

Instead of SHOULDS, it is more helpful and less stressful to look at life in terms of preferences and desires. This perspective is not only reality-based but invites you to employ your limited control to make life work for you as best as you can.

Catastrophizing:

One form of cognitive distortion that can elevate your experience of stress is to perceive life's misfortunes as disasters, or worst-case scenarios. For people who process adversity through a catastrophic lens, undesirable experiences are appraised as utterly unbearable. Needless to say believing that an event is not just problematic or undesirable but an absolute catastrophe needlessly elevates the stress experienced.

Now, this dysfunctional and damaging effect of catastrophic thinking is easy to understand and embrace when applied to examples such as an individual exhibiting absolute rage as a result of being stuck in traffic. In reality, there is a traffic jam, and it is likely that he will be late for his desired appointment. But the stress experienced and the rage manifested suggest that for him this is not merely an inconvenience but rather an absolute catastrophe, a major disaster.

While the irrationality and dysfunctionality of such catastrophic thinking is apparent in an illustration such as this, it is important to note that our own thinking is equally "irrational" and "useless" anytime we go beyond the facts of the moment and distort those facts in a way that colors them as catastrophes and maximizes our stress.

For example, consider the situation where a person notices a black, irregularly shaped mole on his back. It would not be unexpected that such a discovery elevates the individual's level of concern and stress. However, a person who, without further evidence, concludes that this is not only melanoma, but they are now doomed to die would be engaging in catastrophic thinking and maximizing their stress.

When you find yourself engaging in catastrophic thinking, genuinely believing that this or that is "the worst thing ever" or "nothing will ever change," it is essential to determine the facts of what is occurring and keep those separate from your thoughts of what is possible. Knowing "what is" will help you to adjust and adapt to the real (and not imagined) demands you are facing.

Dialing Back Our Stress

Learning to challenge and restructure your faulty thinking and replacing these thoughts with more accurate, reality-based interpretations will help you dial back your stress to a more functional and reasonable level. Being able to stay focused on the facts and refusing to exaggerate, distort, or catastrophize in the face of life demands will require some work, much diligence, and a few simple steps!

SEE THINGS AS THEY ARE

While you may not be as reactive and catastrophic in your thinking as the individual discovering the mole, it is a good bet that you have had moments of elevating, exaggerating, or even catastrophizing life's demands. Have you ever found yourself thinking or saying, "This all too much" or "I can't stand it"? If you have, then at those moments you were distorting the actual task at hand and elevating your stress. After all, you are standing it, and it is not too much to do, and even if by chance it were, why would you stress? The truth, even under these conditions, is that if it can't be done, then why try?

So what is the directive? The directive is to focus on "what is" and nothing more or less. Stick to the facts of the moment. Keeping focused on reality rather than distorting it will help you not to optimize your stress so that you can maximize your ability to adapt.

TAKE A SCIENTIST-RESEARCH VIEW OF LIFE

The suggestion to be grounded in reality and focus on what is also invites you to view your own interpretations of events not as absolute fact, but rather as an initial hypothesis requiring more data to support or reject.

Consider a situation as challenging as receiving a medical diagnosis of having cancer. Yes, the diagnosis and the immediate implications are stressful. This diagnosis will require decisions and adaptation. However, even in this situation, the individual receiving such a diagnosis needs to manage the meaning assigned to that diagnosis. Jumping to the conclusion that this is a death sentence will undoubtedly elevate the stress experienced. And while this conclusion may be a possibility, it is just that, a possibility and not an absolute fact. Recognizing that our interpretations, especially those that are elevating our stress, are hypotheses needing to be tested will direct us to tone down our stress response and turn our attention to gaining the data, the facts we need to develop a more accurate view of what is and what needs to be done.

DE-CATASTROPHIZE

When the source of our excessive and dysfunctional stress response is our use of a catastrophic view of events, we need to de-catastrophize by identifying the most realistic worst-case scenario. Rather than trying to convince yourself that everything will be okay (and it might be), it is sometimes helpful to attempt to identify *the realistic* worst case.

When de-catastrophizing it is helpful to push yourself to ask and answer the question: "So what? What does it mean and how will it affect me if this happens?" The "so what" question is not intended to convey that you don't care, but instead it is a directive to identify possible or probable outcomes. This push toward identifying potential or even likely results will help you to determine the real issues that might have to be addressed, which in turn may help you begin to see practical solutions.

Let's imagine that you are unexpectedly released from your job. What are the real immediate consequences? What are the realistic, probable consequences? Are there financial implications? For example, will you lose your house? Wait—don't answer that.

How could you answer that? Do we know if there is a significant severance package? Do we know about savings? Do we know if there is a mortgage? How about the possibility of a new job? These are just a few of the data points we need to consider before responding. It is hard… but we must control the tendency to jump to catastrophic conclusions.

When our mind starts spinning apocalyptic outcomes, it is crucial for us to ask the "so what" question. So what is the realistic worst-case scenario at the moment and the foreseeable future? Being fired may have been unexpected, it may even be disappointing, but it is not the end of the world, nor is it automatically a definitive statement of significant financial, social, or occupational doom. Losing one's job could raise many questions and concerns about immediate, intermediate, and long-term impact, but it is important to remember that they are questions and not definitions of the inevitable. Knowing this will help you to resist catastrophizing and identify strategies that will help you to adapt to this situation.

Managing Stress: Journaling and Debating

A useful strategy in managing stress is to employ a thought journal (see chapter 2). Placing your thoughts out on paper where you can see them and reprocess them in a way that engages all of your knowledge about the event will help you gain clarity about the actual demands being encountered. This process will help you to challenge your cognitive distortions and reformulate the meaning you place on the event so that it more accurately reflects the reality of the moment.

Give It a Try

To experience the value of this process of recognizing, debating, and reformulating beliefs that are distorting reality and elevating your levels of stress, try the following.

1. Identify a recent time when you experienced an elevated level of stress.

2. Using your journal (see chapter 2) describe the event as accurately as possible (all the significant details).

3. Identify your thoughts that you may have had at the time of the event. What meaning were you assigning to the event or to those involved?

4. In reviewing your interpretations, ask yourself the following:

a. Is the way I am seeing this event factual? Accurate?

b. Am I distorting the event by engaging in catastrophizing?

c. Am I setting unrealistic, perfectionistic standards?

d. Would others who know me and this situation agree to the reasonableness of my worst-case depiction?

e. What could I do to alter the chances of the worst-case prediction and cope with the most likely outcome supported by the data?

5. Now, given your responses to each of the above, rewrite your belief, your interpretation of the event. Is this interpretation more reality-based? Would such a belief position you to be less stressed about the event?

CHAPTER 4

Anxiety: It Is NOT the Things That Go Bump in the Night

If you can solve your problem, then what is the need of worrying?
If you cannot solve it, then what is the use of worrying?
—Shantideva (eighth-century Buddhist monk)

GHOSTS, GHOULS, MONSTERS, beasts, and of course the Bogey (or if you prefer Boogie) man have for most of us been identified as the source of our nightly fears. Many children who give voice to being afraid of the dark are, as we now understand, not at all afraid of the dark. It is not the dark that serves as the source of their anxiety but rather the things that they place in the dark—things they believe "go bump in the night."

It would be nice if our self-created, anxiety-provoking monsters died in childhood. They don't. Rather than the monsters of childhood, we generate all our own worst-case scenarios of life with our "what could be" or "what could have happened." Just as children create dysfunctional anxiety (not all anxiety is dysfunctional, as will be discussed), adults are prone to creating anxiety that neither serves their emotional well-being nor optimally prepares them for coping with real danger.

Anxiety—What and Why?

The experience we identify as anxiety is the result of a complicated set of bodily reactions which are geared to help us cope with real danger. As you are aware, when anxious your adrenaline system ramps up, and with it comes many physical effects. The adrenaline secreted at the time of danger results in our heightened respiration and heart rate. There is a general increase in the blood flow and oxygen to our major muscle groups and essential organs. At the same time, nonessential systems such as our gastrointestinal system are shut down (thus our feeling of nausea). All of these physical changes are in preparation for either fighting off the danger or fleeing from it. This response has been identified as a fight-flight response and is intended to help us survive extreme danger.

While anxiety is undoubtedly discomforting, it has value in helping us maintain our well-being when under attack. The problem arises when the threat or danger is not real or is not as threatening as we believe. Under these conditions, we may find that our anxiety is at a level that is not only discomforting but is actually interfering with our ability to cope.

The Role of "ME" in the Creation of Anxiety

It could be said that we are hardwired to respond to danger with this adrenaline response or anxious state. However, the fact that we have evolved such a protective system does not mean we are an inactive, noncontributing element to the experience, with little control over it.

We are not passive victims of anxiety. For anxiety to occur, it must be triggered by our belief that we are in imminent danger. It is our belief that the situation we are in poses a danger, a threat, to our well-being that serves as the source of our anxiety.

If you think about the role our meaning-making plays in the creation of our anxiety, you will realize...we don't even need a specific event to become anxious. We can create anxiety anytime we wish, simply by believing we are in danger.

Think about it. Have you ever sat in a movie theater and found yourself experiencing an elevated anxiety level as you watched the heroine and hero enter a dangerous situation? Here you are in a comfy chair, perhaps with a snack and drink and maybe even with a friend or loved one, and yet you are responding as if you were in danger. Mentally placing yourself into the action on screen will elevate your level of anxiety, and perhaps that contributes to your enjoyment of the movie. If so—then okay, go for it. But when your anxiety is debilitating and interfering with your emotional well-being and functioning, you need to remember that you—and your belief that you are in danger—are creating this response.

Perhaps you know someone, or maybe you are someone, who nearly panics when encountering a garden snake, getting an injection at the doctor's office, or giving a speech. An over-the-top anxiety response to such non-dangerous or minimally threatening situations is not only uncomfortable but can actually interfere with your ability to cope effectively and perform at your best. These are situations in which your anxiety is truly dysfunctional.

So, what is the source for such dysfunctional anxiety?

You guessed it...it is your engagement with cognitive distortions.

Cognitive Distortions and Dysfunctional Anxiety

As is true for all our emotions, anxiety can have a value and a role in our survival: anxiety can position us to defend ourselves in the face of danger. The point to remember, however, is that while your anxiety is a response to danger, that danger is truly in the "eye" (or, more accurately, the thoughts) of you, the beholder.

Given that your interpretations of events can be distortions of the reality of the moment, it is possible that you may perceive danger and threat at times when little to none exist. Is one failing grade truly dangerous? Is that garden snake life-endangering? With the possibility that your beliefs may falsely assign danger to events that are less than dangerous, it is important for you to consider the following questions when experiencing anxiety.

First, ask yourself: *Is the situation or the event one that will cause me harm?* Perhaps the answer to that question will be yes. Perhaps the event does have the potential to harm or in some way threaten your well-being. As such, the second question to consider is: *Is the level of anxiety proportionate to the actual level of danger presented, and does it position me to protect and defend myself effectively?*

Your responses to these questions may highlight the fact that your interpretation of the situation and the meaning you are assigning to it are distorting the event and creating undue and dysfunctional anxiety. In responding to these questions, you will be invited to challenge your appraisal of the anxiety-provoking event and gain a more functional, reality-based view of the level of threat. For such a reappraisal to be effective, you must continue to recognize and correct any cognitive distortions that you may be employing, particularly the tendency to engage in *Fortune-telling* and *Catastrophizing*.

FORTUNE-TELLING:

Fortune-telling is the cognitive error of taking any one of life's many challenges and immediately jumping from "what is" to "what could be." With fortune-telling, you no longer are responding to the actual event. Instead, you are mentally creating a future event that you truly believe has been triggered. It is this self-generated future—one reflecting more danger than is currently encountered—that serves as the source of your anxiety.

You know the situation. There is a message on your phone to call your mother…RIGHT AWAY! Your thoughts? *Oh, God, what's wrong? I hope she hasn't fallen.* Or maybe you receive a letter from the Internal Revenue Service. Your interpretation? *Oh, crap, I am being audited!*

Predicting the future without adequate information is fortune-telling, and when the future is predicted to be bleak, negative, and threatening…anxiety results.

I had a client who would become frozen in fear when told that she had to undergo a medical test involving a magnetic resonance imaging (MRI) procedure. This procedure would require her to be placed on a moveable examination table and gently secured with straps. The straps are employed to help her remain in the correct position throughout the procedure. Now, lying on a hard examining table in one position for an extended period of time (thirty to fifty minutes) can be uncomfortable. It is unpleasant, but it is not dangerous.

For my client, however, the very thought of going

through a tube with a diameter of twenty-four to twenty-eight inches was enough to trigger major anxiety. For her, it was not the actual tight confines, or the slow-moving table, nor even the straps helping to stabilize her body that served as the source of the anxiety. Rather, it was her thoughts, her predictions, about getting stuck and being unable to exit the machine. *Something could go wrong, the machine could catch fire or something, and I wouldn't be able to get out! Or maybe I won't be able to breathe...*

The reality of the situation is that there are attendants present, both ends of the machine are open, and thus there is plenty of oxygen. But this reality was not being considered by my client, and so her fears seemed reasonable. Her anxiety was in response to a situation, a dangerous situation, that she was creating by way of her fortune-telling.

As you might expect, maintaining a functional level of anxiety requires that we stubbornly RESIST jumping to conclusions and rather stay focused on what we know to be true moment to moment. Staying focused on the "what is" will position us to accurately identify the actual threat being presented and with that accurate appraisal engage in a functional anxiety response.

The following exercise ("What Is" vs. "What Could Be") might help to highlight both the ease with which we can engage in such fortune-telling and the needless anxiety we can create.

"What Is" vs. "What Could Be"

Directions: For each of the following situations, create a conclusion or view of the situation that would place it in the category of high threat and danger. Rate the level of anxiety produced by this conclusion. Next, review the situation and, given what is presented, develop a more realistic appraisal of the situation. Record any adjustment to the anticipated level of anxiety.

SITUATION

(example) Going into have my quarterly review with my boss

You have a message from your doctor's office that states: "We have your recent test results and would like you to come into the office to discuss them as soon as possible."

It's snowing, and your teenager is twenty minutes late. He is at the school's basketball game and has the car. He has been driving for only two months.

You have tried to call your elderly relative. You have called and left six messages within the last forty-five minutes. She has not returned your call, which is unusual in that she usually calls right back.

ANXIETY-PROVOKING CONCLUSION

I know I've blown this. This is going to be horrible. Damn, I can't lose this job.

LEVEL OF ANXIETY CREATED

80%

REALISTIC APPRAISAL

My sales are down by 6%, but the department's overall sales are down 12%. This has been a tough quarter for all of us. I would imagine she is not going to be happy and we will have to come up with a strategic plan to improve next quarter's sales.

ADJUSTED LEVEL OF ANXIETY

40%

CATASTROPHIZING:

A double whammy occurs when an individual not only engages in fortune-telling, but the predicted outcome takes the form of the absolute worst-case situation. Catastrophizing is a process in which the individual drastically overestimates the danger of the situation. This might be what you did in the exercise "What Is" vs. "What Could Be."

With catastrophizing, you might start out by making a relatively accurate assessment of the situation. For example, consider the situation of a woman receiving feedback from her doctor regarding her recent mammogram. The doctor notes that while "things look okay, there was some evidence of areas of dense tissue that we should keep an eye on." Upon hearing this news, she thinks: *Dense tissue?*

I think my mom also had dense breast tissue.

Now, if she stopped at this point, her concern and anxiety would most likely serve to remind her to follow up on her appointment while at the same time not disrupting her functioning as she moved on. But if she engaged with catastrophic thinking, she would move from focusing on the details of the events and what she knew about those details to creating predictions of the worst-case outcome. In this case, she would jump from the data identifying dense tissue to the conclusion that she has breast cancer, and perhaps jumping again to the belief that she will surely die.

With catastrophic thinking, we take extreme possibilities, even improbabilities, and embrace them as realities of the moment.

Regardless of the form it takes or the situation in which it is employed, catastrophic thinking results in elevated and dysfunctional anxiety. The person who goes into panic mode when receiving a poor work assessment or one who is overwhelmed with anxiety following the breakup of a relationship is most likely not "seeing" the actual impact of the event but rather jumping to catastrophic conclusions. *That's it, I know I will be fired! What will I do—I can't afford to keep my house. Damn, we won't have health insurance...* or, *I'll never have a relationship! I am going to be alone the rest of my life.* Thoughts such as these reflect catastrophic thinking and serve as the foundation for elevated anxiety.

While these extreme conclusions may be possible, they are NOT in evidence at this point in time. Thus the anxiety they generate is not proportional to the actual threat and fails to help the individual adapt to that situation. This is a core characteristic of dysfunctional anxiety—it not only is disproportionate to the threat being encountered but it also actually blocks adaptive responding.

One client with whom I worked experienced heart palpitations which in turn would trigger his panic response. He described multiple situations where he was merely sitting quietly and would become aware that his heart was "beating funny." Now, while any disruption to a normal heart rhythm should be a point of concern, this client immediately jumped to the worst-case prediction: *Oh, my god, I am having a heart attack. I am going to die, and there is no one here to help.* Interpreting this event through such a catastrophic lens not only failed to help him adjust and adapt to the palpitations but actually increased his symptoms of arousal and elevated his heart rate. With the increase in his anxiety, more thoughts of disaster would occur, and the result was increased anxiety and symptoms of anxiety. This cycle would continue to the point of full-blown panic.

As noted, any deviation from a normal heart rhythm should be a matter of curiosity if not concern. But not all palpitations equate with an imminent heart attack. It is possible that it is the result of too much caffeine or some other less lethal explanation. Until more data are acquired, it does very little good to jump to conclusions, especially when these conclusions are catastrophic.

For our anxiety to be useful, the level experienced

should be proportional to the actual level of threat presented in order to prepare us to defend ourselves in the face of
that threat. In this case, my client was feeling some unusual heart rhythm (versus dying at the moment). Further, his
awareness of this arrhythmia and the anxiety experienced
should have served as the motivation for contacting his
physician. Jumping to the immediate conclusion that he
was in the grip of a heart attack failed to serve as a useful
motivator. It merely placed him in a state of panic, unable
to focus or function.

Get a Grip

For your anxiety to be of use in the maintenance of your
well-being, you will need to develop an approach to assessing life events as they are—without exaggeration. You
truly need to increase your ability to get a grip on things *as
they are*, identifying the facts of an event as distinct from
your interpretations of those facts and your predictions of
what it may mean for your current and future well-being.

When you are anxious, you need to do a reality check.
When anxious you believe that the situation is threatening
and the consequence will be dangerous. You need to question this, not reject it or deny it—examine its validity. You
need to remember that your beliefs, your thoughts, and
your interpretations are initial hypotheses and not absolute facts. The way you interpret events needs to be tested
against the actual data being presented. When anxious
you will do well to ask yourself: *Is the situation actually as*

harmful and as dangerous as I believe?

Let the Debating and the Reformulating Begin

When in the grip of anxiety, it may be difficult to accurately assess facts that support the notion that you are in danger, as well as facts that help you identify the level of present danger and the various options for reducing that danger. However, through practice, even practice of reflecting on previous experiences and challenging your original perspective on those experiences, you will increase your ability to engage in this process of rational thinking. It requires practice to "get a grip" and maintain a realistic view of life's challenge and stubbornly refuse to distort the level of threat being presented. The following exercise invites you to reflect on a recent event or encounter to which you responded with a high level of anxiety, and engage in the debating and reformulating processes.

FACTS VS. INTERPRETATIONS

Directions: Use your multi-column journal to identify your beliefs about the situation, identify fortune-telling and catastrophic thinking and determine if they have been employed, and reformulate your interpretation of the situation so that it more accurately reflects the degree of immediate threat and danger. Complete each of the following.

1. Identify a recent time when you experienced a

high level of anxiety.

2. Write out a complete description of the event; list
    only the actual details and not your judgments of
    those details.

3. Identify the thoughts you may have had at the time
    of the event. How were you interpreting it? What
    meaning were you assigning to the event or to
    those involved?

4. In reviewing your interpretations and thoughts, ask
    yourself the following:

    a. Did my thoughts accurately reflect the event or
        did they include some fortune-telling (jumping
        to conclusions)?

    b. If I predicted some conclusion or outcome, is
        it a reasonable extension of the facts or am I
        going to a worst-case scenario?

    c. Is my conclusion probable, or merely possible?
        Is it out of the realm of possibility?

    d. d. How might another person interpret the lev-
        el of threat or danger being presented?

5. Now, given your responses to each of the above,
    rewrite your belief, your interpretation of the event.
    Is this interpretation more reality-based? Would
    such a belief position you to be less anxious about
    the event?

Practicing this process of identifying the meaning you
are assigning a situation, testing this belief against the facts,
and adjusting to bring your thoughts more in line with the

realities of the moment will make this process almost automatic. Yes, it takes practice and time, but you are worth the effort. The impact will be to increase your ability to deal with life's threats and challenges in a way that maximizes your emotional well-being.

CHAPTER 5

Anger: It's Not You…It's Me Who's Pissing Me Off!

It is a waste of time to be angry about my disability. One has to get on with life, and I haven't done badly. People won't have time for you if you are always angry or complaining.

—Stephen Hawking (1942–2018*)*

I CAN REMEMBER a client who was ordered by the court to come to counseling because of an incident of road rage that endangered him and others. The specific event happened while he was waiting to drive around a roadblock. My client became extremely angry when another driver, according to my client, "broke ranks and rushed ahead of me at the detour lane." Believing that this other driver was not abiding by the rules of roadblock navigation, my client passed the roadblock, raced his car ahead of the other driver, pulled in front, and came to a rapid stop. Luckily the other driver stopped before crashing into my client's car. With both cars stopped, my client jumped out of his car and climbed on the hood of the other car, jumped up and down, damaging the hood, and then proceeded to kick in the front windshield. All because this other driver "broke ranks…"

Anger, as a response to an attack or as a response to frustration, can be a useful source of energy and motivation to help push us toward our goals. However, anger such as that exhibited by this client is clearly unhealthy and potentially dangerous for all involved. While it would be a relief to believe that this type of rage was highly unusual and infrequent, a quick review of the daily news headlines would suggest otherwise.

Hopefully, you have not experienced anger and manifested rage at an extreme degree. But it is very likely that you can identify situations where your anger was neither proportional to the actual level of threat, nor useful in helping you adapt to the situation and meet your needs. Have you ever screamed at an erratic driver who perhaps came too close to your car, or yelled at a driver who was failing to move on a green light? Maybe you have slammed your fist on a table or kicked or hit a vending machine, or maybe threw a toy on which you almost tripped. In retrospect, were these forms of anger necessary to adapt to these situations? Did the arousal of anger at these moments contribute to your well-being? If not, then let's face it, they were moments of dysfunctional (and if you will allow "crazy") anger.

We all get angry, and sometimes that anger is less than functional. So, what are we to do?

Combating Our Anger: Vent? Repress? Or...?

Working for over forty years in clinical practice, I had numerous clients for whom explosive anger was a problem. Few exhibited the rage of the client depicted in the opening of this chapter, and most found that their anger took form in verbal explosions. But in all of these cases, the client was able to identify the cost that their anger had on their work or their relationships.

Many of these clients had previously gone for counseling or therapy and had often received help in developing strategies for managing the anger and the various costly forms of expression. Some were encouraged to suppress their anger ("bite your tongue") whereas others were helped to express their anger in less damaging ways—hitting a pillow, screaming into their hands, or pounding clay.

Now, assuming these strategies help prevent the individual from doing harm to self, others, or property, they have value. What I found interesting, however, was that all too often the directive for those with anger issues was for them to learn how to control or redirect their anger rather than to learn how to STOP CREATING their dysfunctional anger.

We are ACTIVE creators of our emotion, and that includes our anger. Anger, like all emotions, is self-generated. Anger is NOT an IT. Anger is a YOU! It truly is not the other person or this or that situation that is causing your anger…it is you!

Thinking My Way into Anger

Take a moment and look at the language we use when angry. We say things like "Damn you (or it)," or "You (or it) make me want to scream," or the classic… "You really piss me off." These phrases are not empty. They reflect a belief that our anger is in response to some external situation or event.

While we have been conditioned to believe that our anger is an involuntary response to unjust, unfair life events, the truth is that our anger is the result of *our belief* that we are experiencing something which we deem as unfair and unjust. That may seem like a minor distinction… It is not.

Life can throw a lot of unexpected and undesirable circumstances at you. The fact that your car battery is dead, or your appointment failed to show, or even that someone took the last parking spot close to your building may be undesirable, but is it directly connected to an anger response? Situations you see as undesirable are merely that—undesirable situations and nothing more. For an undesirable situation to be one to which you respond with anger, you will need to see these events as genuinely *unjust* and believe that *you are unfairly under attack*. It is this belief that creates the anger you experienced.

Your anger is in fact self-generated. People don't and in fact can't piss you off. YOU piss you off by believing that what you are experiencing is unfair, unjust, and simply not the way it is supposed to be. I know this is countercultural, and most people you meet will definitely give the responsibility (and the power) for their anger to another. Believing that your anger is an automatic, "natural" response to a life event or another person's actions or comments is not only an extension of the "big lie" (that our emotions are externally created) but it is a belief that interferes with your ability to respond to these less-than-desirable situations successfully.

This doesn't mean we need to surrender all anger. Anger, as is true for all of your emotions, can have value in some situations. Anger can serve as a source of energy and motivation to help us maintain our safety and/or push us toward our goals. The question is not *Should I or shouldn't I be angry,* but rather *Does my anger in this situation and at this level of intensity serve me well?*

Irritated, Annoyed, but Not Raging

For your anger, irritation, and annoyance to be useful, you will need to be able to recognize and avoid the "crazies" (i.e., cognitive distortions) that lead to elevated and dysfunctional levels of anger and rage. The cognitive distortions often serving in the creation of dysfunctional anger include "shoulding," mind-reading, labeling, and magnification.

SHOULDING (THERE ARE NO MUSTS OR SHOULD...JUST "IS")

I worked with a client who came to counseling in an attempt to learn how to better "deal" with her mother-in-law. The client admitted that she was continuously angry with her mother-in-law, and she was quick to justify the anger with illustrations of all of her mother-in-law's "terrible" behavior. The client provided numerous illustrations of what she felt were her mother-in-law's manipulative behaviors. She shared about the time when she was chastised by the mother-in-law for giving a particular wedding gift, and the Easter dinner where the mother-in-law was critical of the place settings, or the time when she was invited to the mother-in-law's for dinner and all she was served were cold cuts. She was willing and able to share numerous illustrations of behaviors that she felt were apparent violations of how a mother-in-law should act. The list of incidents that she used as evidence was extensive and, in my client's mind, clear justification for her ongoing irritation and anger.

At one point in our session, I summarized all the "evidence" presented against the mother-in-law and asked my client if this was a change in her mother-in-law or if she had been like this for some time. My client responded by saying: "I have been married for twelve years, and she has been like this since day one. She was even critical of the music we picked for our wedding."

I asked: "Given that this is how she has been for the past twelve years, why do you get angry when she does those things that by now you expect?"

Her response was not only definitive but insightful (at least for me). "Why? Because she has no right being that way!"

Think about that. The mother-in-law had no right being the person she was, with the choices she made and the behaviors she exhibited. From my client's perspective, the mother-in-law's actions were not merely undesirable; they were not allowed. They were violations of some code of behavior for mothers-in-law, and as such her mother-in-law should be condemned for such violation. This, of course, would make sense IF my client made up the rules for the world.

Taking my client's perspective of her mother-in-law, one could begin to understand her anger. After all, if her mother-in-law, in fact, had no right acting the way she did, and yet she continued to violate this absolute rule, wasn't my client's anger justified? The problem with this perspective is that the rules the mother-in-law is apparently breaking are those created by my client and may not be understood or shared.

When observing the actions of others, it is tempting to impose our own standards of right and wrong and view their actions through our lens of what *should* or *must* be done. It is a case where our personal preferences have now become the commandments or the law for all humanity.

Using words such as *should have* or *must* may reflect our perspective of demanding that someone act, think, or even feel a certain way. Thoughts such as *That person should hurry up*, or *He is so unfair, it's not right*, or even *How rude, she has no right to say that*, all reflect a rigid standard of what is and what is not appropriate. It is a subjective and personal standard that is imposed as if it were universal. Believing that this absolute rule has been violated invites us to feel righteous and justified in exhibiting our anger, dismay, or complete rejection of the other. With this as our mind-set, we will find the situation more than merely unacceptable; it will be intolerable, and the individuals will be seen as awful when they don't adhere to these "laws."

Perhaps you had moments of anger when you thought:

- What the hell is wrong with that jerk?
- That bitch! She can't get away with that!
- This is so unfair!
- Move it, what are you waiting for!
- Hey, that's my parking spot! (or I was here first!)

If you review each of the above, you may see a pattern. Underlying each statement is the belief that ***the world shouldn't be like this!*** Further, it is highly likely that if you or I made up the rules for the world, it would not be like this. However, the truth is that we don't!

While it may sound crazy to believe that we are the one and only ruler of the universe, it is precisely this type of thinking, this fundamental belief, that is operative when we are Musting and Shoulding and, as a result, positioning ourselves for...raging!

Now, this is not to suggest that we don't have a right to develop our own standards of behavior. It is also not being suggested that it may be true that if one would act according to my rules, it may prove beneficial for all. The point is to remember that there is no SHOULD or MUST but only what is and what is desirable (at least for me). With this as a perspective, a person would be motivated to figure out how to make the situation more aligned with what they desired, rather than engaging with anger.

Perhaps the following personal example may help to clarify the dysfunctionality of such "shoulding."

It was a beautiful Saturday morning, and I was mowing my lawn. As I was working, I noticed that my eldest son was awake and watching television. I continued to mow the lawn, and as I did, I found myself becoming annoyed. I was working myself up with thoughts such as: *What is he doing? He SHOULD be out here helping me!* The more I processed this situation through my list of what he Should-Must be doing, the more annoyed (dare I say angry) I became.

Now, having practiced cognitive therapy for years, I find that it is hard for me to get away with my own crazies for too long. So as I was mowing and recognizing my increasing annoyance, I focused in on my thinking. Boy, I had a long list of shoulds and musts going on in my head. *He shouldn't be watching television. He should care about this property and how it looks. He should be more sensitive to my needs.* You get the idea. But as I listened to these thoughts, I heard (faintly) the rational side of me ask a simple question: *Why should he?*

Ouch. Trust me, I tried my best to come up with the evidence that my "shoulds" were valid. But the more I debated, the more I realized a couple of points. First, I was mowing the lawn because I wanted to. I know—I tried to argue that the lawn had to be mowed, but the truth is it didn't have to be…it was simply something I preferred. The world wouldn't stop, and nothing drastic would impact my life if I stopped mowing. I just didn't like the way it looked, so I was doing what I wanted. I wanted to make it look a certain way. That point led me to the next insight.

My son, like me, was doing what he wanted. Doing what one wants is not a violation of an absolute rule; it is in service of that person's interest. So accepting the fact that we were both choosing to engage in activities that were meeting our needs or interest at the moment allowed me to diffuse my irritation, my annoyance. But how about the lawn?

Well, that was another insight that I discovered. The fact that I was choosing to mow the lawn didn't mean that I wouldn't have enjoyed some help. I still wanted my son to come out and help.

The awareness that he was choosing to do something he wished to do, and I wanted him to do something that apparently was not as appealing, directed me to think of ways to motivate him to help. Fortunately, this time around, all it took was for me to ask him. No need to feel anger. No need to act angry. Just ask for help.

Combatting the use of shoulding and musting in processing your experience will require you to identify their presence and then strongly remind yourself of the subjectivity to these rules. It is important to tell yourself that your view, your rule, your preference is not universal nor is it sacred. There are no MUSTS or SHOULDS, just merely your preferences and desires for the way you would like it to be.

In combating the damage of such thinking, it is important to accept the reality that people choose to act in ways that, at least at the moment, appear to be most desirable to them. With this perspective, you will be able to accept the reality that there are times when others will behave in ways that are intended to be self-serving and not *you*-serving. This is reality, and embracing this reality places you in a position of deciding how to increase the possibility of your needs being met, rather than exploding in dysfunctional anger.

MIND READING

I had a client who was a professional reporter. During one of our sessions, he seemed preoccupied and a bit annoyed. I invited him to share how he was feeling and what he was thinking about. After apologizing for his distraction, he stated that he was at a news conference before coming to his session, and throughout the entire time, the presenter selected questions from numerous reporters but never him. "He was recognizing people all around me, and he even looked directly at me and then asked the woman behind me for her question. It really pissed me off."

It was obvious that my client was furious. The source of his anger was that he "knew" he was "...deliberately being ignored and shunned" by the presenter.

Neither of us truly knew the intent of the presenter. In addition, there was nothing my client could point to that would suggest there was animus between the presenter and himself. He also was able to admit that in the past he has had many of his questions accepted and answered by the same presenter. Thus while it was possible that the presenter was deliberately ignoring my client's questions, there was no direct evidence that it was true. But the evidence isn't needed when one mind reads.

As was evident in this situation, anger can be flamed by our assuming the hostile intentions of another. When someone behaves in a manner that is against our "rules," we arbitrarily decide that we "know" their motives. We decide that we can read their minds and that they intend to do us harm!

While it may be legitimate to suggest that specific behaviors provide clues to what another is thinking, these clues are just that—hints and not definitive indications. When we move from a possible clue to what another is thinking to concluding that we definitely know what the other is thinking, we are committing the cognitive distortion of *mind reading*. When our mind reading leads us to conclude that the person's behavior was intentionally employed as an attack or threat to *us*, feeling anger is the result.

If you find that mind reading is one of your own crazies, challenge your thinking by considering each of the following.

- What are you predicting the other person is thinking?
- What is your evidence supporting this prediction?
- Would that evidence, if applied to your actions, ALWAYS indicate hostile intentions on your part?
- Is there any evidence (information about the person and the behavior) that is non-supportive of your prediction?
- If we assume your predictions are accurate, that the individual has hostile intentions as the base of their actions, what does that say about them?
- Even if the predictions are accurate, does your level of anger serve you well?

In responding to each of the above, you may experience a reappraisal and reframing of your interpretation of the event and the other person's action which will result in a reduction of your anger and aggression. This was certainly true for my client, who through our discussion was able to identify that this same presenter: (1) took questions from less than half of those in attendance; (2) apologized for the limited time available for the conference; (3) had on more than one past occasion fielded my client's questions; (4) was actually very friendly and sociable with my client following the meeting; and (5) invited all of those in attendance (including my client) to contact him or his office if they had follow-up questions. These new data helped my client reformulate his thoughts about the presenter's hostile intent and, as a result, reduce his irritation.

LABELING

When encountering someone behaving in a manner I find unacceptable, I can elevate my irritation and anger by moving away from the evaluation of the specific event and behavior to an assessment of the person and the person's character. When we label we typically move from seeing this as a single "offensive" event to a belief that the individual perpetrating the event is a "jerk," "idiot," "loser," or even "asshole."

Our labeling invites us to employ sweeping, often negative and inflammatory judgments not just about a person's behavior, but about them as people. No longer do we see someone who cut ahead of us in line; we see a real SOB.

As with most cognitive distortions, the best way to combat this distortion is to get grounded in the reality of the situation. It is essential to redirect our attention, our focus, to the specific actions or inactions that we are finding irritating. To reduce the labeling and with it the elevation of our anger, it is helpful to consider each of the following.

- What is going on? What are the actual facts of the event?
- How does it directly impact me?
- Am I making a judgment about the behavior or making judgments about the person?

If we find that we are doing the latter, then we need to challenge ourselves with one more question:

- Upon what do I base that personal, derogatory judgment?
- Is there information that fails to support my derogatory judgment?
- How does focusing on the person rather than the behavior help me get what I want?

When you refocus on the facts of the moment, the behaviors being exhibited, rather than drawing a general dismissal of the person, you will not only reduce the anger you experience, but you will be in a position that will allow you to work toward getting what you want.

MAGNIFICATION (OUR OLD FRIEND CATASTROPHIZING/AWFULIZING)

We are going to experience points of frustration in our life. Events, circumstances, and people will not always be the way we would prefer them to be. With such frustration comes irritation and even aggression. However, when we take these experiences and give them disproportionate weight and importance, our frustration and anger will increase beyond what is called for in this situation. The incidents of road rage that are reported almost daily, when viewed with a lens targeting the facts of the situation, often reveal the triggers were events as innocuous as someone cutting in line at the toll booth, or turning into a lane without first signaling. The reality of these events does not support the extreme and often lethal responses demonstrated. In each case, the anger displayed is the result of magnifying the event and catastrophizing its impact.

When combating the tendency to catastrophize, it is helpful to:

- Make an honest, realistic—almost scientific—assessment of what is going on and what (real) consequences are occurring or will occur.
- Resist using hyperbolic language in describing the situation. Rather than this is "horrible" or "intolerable," it is more useful and accurate to employ terms such as "unfortunate," "undesirable," or "unexpected."
- Search for any positives to be gained in the situation. Even in times of frustration and disappointment, there may be a positive to be found.
- Admit that it is frustrating. Recognize that when we don't get something we desired, frustration can result. That is legitimate, and it may even be undesirable, but remind yourself you can handle it.
- See the situation as a problem to be resolved—not

a catastrophe to endure.

Taming the Crazies

I think it is fair to assume that there was a time, maybe a very brief moment, where you in fact "lost it." It was a time when your anger was disproportionate to the situation and failed to serve you in the best way. While that incident may have long passed, the way you make meaning and interpret frustrating events remains. It is helpful in defeating your crazies to reflect on moments of dysfunctional anger (even those long past), identify the cognitive distortions that were operative, and develop the pattern of debating and reformulating those thoughts so that they are more rational and functional.

The following exercise invites you to reflect on such incidents and practice the debating and reformulating needed to gain control over your "crazies."

"Okay, So I Lost It"

Directions: Identify an event associated with a time that you became angry (perhaps even lost it) and describe the event in detail. Next, as you review the event, attempt to list all the "self-talk" going on that reflected your belief about the event and those involved. Describe the level of anger experienced (0-100, where 100 is ballistic). Next, use the questions listed below to help you identify cognitive distortions operating with this event and reformulate your thinking so that it is more in line with the facts of the moment. Assuming that the debate resulted in a new per-spective and a different interpretation of the event, write that interpretation and re-score the level of anger with that reframed perspective.

The Event:

_____

_____

_____

_____

The Beliefs (self-talk, interpretation of the event):

_____

_____

_____

_____

Feelings (the consequence of your interpretation):

_____

_____

_____

_____

(score)_____

Debate: Review your thoughts, your interpretations of the event, and challenge your initial thinking by asking the following questions.

a. Did your thoughts accurately reflect the event or did they include some mind reading? If so—do you really know the intent of the other(s) involved? What are the facts (list them) versus your conclusions?

b. In reviewing the situation, was it as serious as you interpreted or was the process of magnification engaged? If magnification was employed, again simply return to the event, listing only the facts as is and as would be experienced by anyone else.

c. Does your interpretation of the event reflect the imposition of your "shoulds" or "musts"? While the event or the person's actions may not be what you desired, are they, in fact, a violation of some absolute rule? Is it possible that the others involved don't hold similar "rules" of engagement? If so...would there be a more potentially beneficially way of meeting your needs, rather than engaging in anger?

Reformulation: Given your responses to each of the above—rewrite your belief, your interpretation of the event. Is this interpretation more reality-based, more reflective of the facts as others would confirm? Would such a view—such a way of interpreting the event—position you to be less angry about the event?

While the example you employed in completing the exercise may be one that has long passed and for which your original anger has dissipated, remember that a significant value in performing this exercise is that you are not only addressing a specific incident but are also developing the habit of rational thinking—a habit that will defeat your crazies.

CHAPTER 6

Shame and Guilt (Little, If Any, Value)

To err proves human; to forgive leaves you sane and realistic.
—Albert Ellis, 1957

"I CAN'T BELIEVE I did that. I am such a crap. I am so embarrassed I can never go back."

So announced my client as she reflected on her, dare I say, uninhibited and overly friendly behavior at the company Christmas party. She truly was wrecked with an overwhelming sense of shame and guilt. So much so that she thought about quitting her job rather than accept the truth of how she acted, apologize if she so desired, and then develop a plan to modify the behavior she felt was so inappropriate.

Shame and guilt are two emotions that may have some

value in enforcing the rules of conduct in our society, but all too often they are merely sources of unnecessary upset. I would be surprised if you have navigated life without some experience of shame and guilt. Maybe it was in response to accidentally breaking another's special figurine or discovering that you failed to replace the thing you borrowed from your neighbor. Perhaps it was something more involved like sleeping with a friend's significant other, or stealing something of value. Regardless of the specifics it is highly likely that you have, at least once, found yourself in violation of your standards and those of society. If you have, it is not unusual if you have had moments of guilt and, if "caught," shame.

The What and Why of Shame and Guilt

Guilt and shame seem to serve a similar purpose in that they are used to correct what is perceived to be socially inappropriate behavior. But these two emotions are initiated from two different sources.

Guilt is typically the result of *our* judging *our* action, or inaction, as a violation of our values, or accepted norms. The focus of guilt is on our behavior. While comedians have used the concept of Catholic and Jewish guilt as springboards to many careers, the gut-wrenching impact of guilt can be anything but funny.

Shame can also be gut-wrenching. It differs from guilt in that it is the result of external evaluation and feedback. The feelings of distress you experience when shamed are the result of the way those around you react. It is in the process of being caught in the act that you now experience shame. Once you embrace this external evaluation and make it your own, you will experience the negative feelings that result from being disgraced.

When considering the usefulness of these emotional reactions, it would appear that at best we could argue that in a moderate amount and perhaps in the short term both shame and guilt may help to reinforce the rules of civil society. The discomfort that accompanies both shame and guilt can serve as a measure of the need to change things in one's life or one's behavior, and this can be a good thing. Thus if I were to make an off-color comment, one that elicited a negative response from companion, the distress I feel as a result of my guilt and shame could motivate me to apologize for my actions and become more mindful of my speech.

While both shame and guilt, may—and that is a big *may*—have value in helping you correct behavior that you and society deem as undesirable, problems can occur when the shame or the guilt no longer targets a specific action or "transgression" but is applied to you as a person (rather than your actions). It would be the case where I am not merely feeling guilty or ashamed about my comment, but instead, I believe that as a result of this type of behavior, I am really a horrible person and can't face another. I am not just feeling bad and guilty about my behavior but am now feeling ashamed of who and what I am.

I once had a thirteen-year-old client who attempted

suicide in response to his extreme sense of shame. This young man was struggling with his gender identity. In a time when his guard was down, he told his best friend about some of his fantasies about dressing like a girl. Sadly, his friend chose to share the stories on social media, which went viral and resulted in a barrage of cruel verbal attacks on my client. In addition to these social media attacks, my client received numerous handwritten notes and pictures with derogatory graphics and comments.

The reaction he received resulted in intense feelings of shame. In response, he began to withdraw from all his social activities, spent much of his time in his bedroom, and showed signs of depression. His parents had noticed the radical change in his emotions and behavior and encouraged him to speak to his counselor, where he not only shared his story but also expressed his feelings of intense shame and thoughts of suicide.

Here was a thirteen-year-old who was clearly struggling with a significant developmental issue regarding gender identification. Sadly, the external assessment he received stimulated intense guilt over his fantasies and shame about being a person with such fantasies. Now he was not just struggling with his gender identity but shamed into a negative self-assessment and self-hatred. For this client the onslaught of negative messages and resulting shame served as his basis for concluding that he was a disgrace to his family, ultimately unlovable, and that his life was doomed, forever being a social outcast.

Incidents of such devastating impacts of excessive guilt

and shame are not restricted to children and teens. This was brought home to me by a father of a sixteen-year-old who was killed in a traffic accident. This father gave form to the devastating impact of excessive guilt and the resulting depression and self-hatred that resulted.

In meeting with this client, it soon became clear that he took full responsibility for his son's death. From his perspective, he decided to allow his son to drive that fateful night, and that was the sole source of this tragedy. He firmly believed that he should have known better than to let his son drive the car that night. This dad took full responsibility for the death even though the details of the accident revealed that it was neither his nor his son's fault.

The facts of the accident and his son's death were genuinely exceptional. While his son waited at an intersection for the light to turn green, a huge tree simply uprooted, falling on and crushing the car and the boy. The accident was indeed a freak occurrence. Apparently, an extensive period of rain in the area had not only made the tree top heavy but had significantly loosened the ground to allow the tree to uproot without warning. It was clear that no one could have foreseen such an event, nor prevented it from happening. These facts, however, did not assuage the father's guilt. He had convinced himself that he should have known better. That he shouldn't have let his son drive. That it was all his fault. This intense guilt contributed to his grieving in a way that put him into a major depression.

While it is clear that guilt and shame may prove useful for maintaining the rules of conduct for a civilized society, they also can be the source of unnecessary and even devastating emotional upset. It is at these times that we need to reappraise our guilt and shame, viewing it through a lens of rationality.

Regret...Okay. Shame and Guilt...Not So Much

Have you ever told an off-color joke that clearly was not seen as funny? Maybe you got caught telling a lie. Have you ever said or done something that really was not appropriate? If so, then there is a good chance you have intimate knowledge of the emotions of shame and guilt and the discomfort they can cause.

To benefit from the discomfort you feel at moments of social transgressions, you will need to learn to shift your focus away from a negative, demeaning evaluation of yourself to engaging in a realistic assessment of your actions.

Let's assume, for example, that you are caught coming on to your colleague's spouse at the office party. When confronted you process the event as: *Oh my god, what am I doing? This is not in line with how I want to be. I am really sorry.* The remorse felt at the moment reflects your assessment of your actions as undesirable according to your standards. Having fallen short of your standards, you may now find yourself motivated to not only apologize but commit (at least at the moment) to monitor your drinking and party behavior. If this is the process and the outcome, one could argue, the discomfort of shame and guilt was productive. But what happens if upon being caught you conclude: *I am such a crud. I am such a disgusting individual for doing such perverted acts. I will never be able to face my colleague again.* The evaluation now shifts from the action to you as a person. The level of shame, guilt, and emotional discomfort generated by this interpretation appears disproportionate to the event and social violation. But beyond this, believing that you are a crud, a disgusting human being who could never again face your colleague, would result in behavior that is less than functional. With this as your self-evaluation, you might engage in behavior such as going out of your way to avoid contact with the coworker or becoming engulfed in self-hatred. Neither of these responses helps to either reconcile the previous social violation or position you to avoid a similar transgression in the future.

Employing a distorted view of you and your behavior can result in extreme self-downing and self-denigration and lead to depression, social anxiety, and obsession about the events. Under these conditions, it is less likely that you will own up to the act and attempt to make amends or engage in strategies to prevent a repeat of the behavior. From such a self-downing position, your energy will be redirected to behavior that mires you in self-downing or ineffectual practices, such as avoiding ownership of the action, denial of the action, or even overcompensating for the apparent wrongdoing.

When our social transgressions are filtered through cognitive errors (aka our craziness) such as DEMANDING

(I shouldn't have done that) and SELF-DOWNING (I'm such a horrible person), the result is not the creation of emotions that motivate personal growth but rather emotions that are damaging to our effective functioning and well-being. Given the destructive quality of these cognitive distortions, it is vital to understand them, recognize them when they are operative, and learn to challenge and reformulate them.

DEMANDING: The Shoulds and Musts in Service of Guilt and Shame

I am not sure either shame or guilt could exist without embracing the many "shoulds" and "musts" that occupy our thoughts. Believing that my actions or inactions are in violation of some sacred set of "shoulds" and "musts" invites my self-reprimands in the form of shame and guilt. Truly believing that you "shouldn't have done it" establishes an experience that is neither instructive nor productive and is, in fact, unrealistic and illogical. The truth of the matter is…you did do it. Demanding that you shouldn't have neither changes the actual event nor positions you to learn from it.

There is no MUST or SHOULD involved with the incident of your concern. The event and your actions simply occurred. Yes, the truth is that you did something which now in retrospect you wish you had done differently. The operative words here are "in retrospect."

The actions and behaviors in which you engaged now

are viewed as undesirable or ill-serving. It is just in hind-sight that you now wish you had done something different-ly. The fact is that your behavior made sense to you at that time. Think about it. You didn't look at the situation and, given the details of the moment, decide, "Let me do some-thing that is totally inappropriate and outside the boundar-ies of my social standards." It is now, only with the luxury of being able to look back on the situation, that you see all the options (to which you were blind at the time). It is now, with this new broader perspective, that you now unreason-ably put yourself down for not choosing one of these alter-natives. Yes, hindsight is 20/20. We neither have the gift of hindsight nor should be punished for failing to employ it.

I remember one client sharing a story of her guilt about "coming on" to a married man. She explained that she was at a professional conference, and following one of the meetings, she went to the hotel bar for a cocktail. While there, she noticed a man wearing a name tag that indi-cated he was attending the same conference. She took her drink over to introduce herself, and the two began to share their experience with the conference. After about an hour of conversing and another drink (or perhaps two), she found herself being somewhat flirtatious. She could not remember the specific circumstances, but at some point in their conversation, the man looked at his watch and excused himself, saying: "I apologize. I was supposed to meet with my wife ten minutes ago in the restaurant. Perhaps the three of us could catch up after dinner?" She told the story in total embarrassment, stating that she felt "wretched" coming on to a married man. From her point of view, she "...should never have done such an act."

To her surprise, I had to agree. Given her standards and her desire to live by those standards, she certainly shouldn't have come on to a married man. The problem with this thinking, as applied to this situation, is that she is using hindsight to punish herself. Her guilt and self-downing reflect her unrealistic perspective on what she should have done, when in fact it was something she could not have done. At the time she had no indication that he was married.

Perhaps in reflecting on a moment of guilt or shame, you also can look in retrospect and wish that you had acted differently. However, engaging in SHOULD thinking is denying the reality that you couldn't have acted differently. You did what you did at the moment, and that moment has passed.

Think about it.

The guilt-ridden and shameful you believes "I shouldn't have done that! I should have known better." The rational functional you believes "Wow, knowing what I know now, I would have done this rather than that" or even, "In looking back, I can see it would have been preferable if I had done this rather than that." There is a benefit to using your ability to look back and process an event to learn from it. There is no benefit to using your ability to look back to make yourself feel guilty for not knowing then what you know now.

It is clear that accepting the fact that you, like I, are a

fallible human being—who by definition of that fallibility will at times act in ways that you or others deem less than desirable—will position us to avoid the damaging effects of guilt and shame. Rather than placing unreasonable demands for perfect adherence to subjective standards, it is more functional and more helpful to your emotional well-being to accept your fallibility and process your "failings" through the lens of "*It would be better* (more desirable, preferable) if…" rather than a rigid lens of musts and shoulds. By refusing to "should" on yourself, and allowing yourself to embrace your fallibility and your ability to learn from mistakes, you will be positioned to learn from the experience and respond differently the next time a similar experience is presented.

SELF-DOWNING

Okay, so let's assume you did perform an action that was short of your standards and therefore less than desirable. What does this say about you as a person, as a human being?

People experiencing extreme guilt too often engage in a cognitive error by which they use their behavior or actions as evidence that they are inadequate or flawed human beings. Too often, those with extreme guilt use their failings as a rationale for self-downing.

This was the case with my client, whom I will call Jacob, a twenty-seven-year-old medical student who recently experienced the death of his grandmother. Jacob explained that he was having difficulty sleeping and concentrating on his school work. "I just feel horrible. I know she was ninety-seven, but she was all alone in her house—which is only two blocks from my school." As Jacob shared his story, it became clear that he was experiencing extreme guilt over the fact that while his grandmother lived only two blocks from school, he had failed to visit her during the week that she passed.

He was very clear about how he failed as a grandson. "I should have been there. She was a super lady, and I really should have given her more attention." Holding on to the belief that he was an unloving, uncaring grandson set the stage for extreme self-downing and rumination, which were now interfering with his ability to function. "I shouldn't have been so self-absorbed. She died all alone. Why didn't I stop over?"

His pain, his anguish, and his guilt were real. Sadly, these feelings were generated by his belief in his violation of irrational "shoulds" and "musts." As his story unfolded, it became clear that he demonstrated a concern and interest in his grandmother, as evidenced by the fact that he scheduled lunch with her once a week. Further, the scene that he painted and imposed on himself regarding her dying alone did not match the reality of the moment. Through our discussion he revealed that his grandmother had a live-in nurse, whom she adored and who he felt was very sweet, loving, and competent.

We will never know the experience that Jacob's grandmother encountered as she passed away, but we do know that the specific facts of the event do not immediately support Jacob's beliefs that somehow he had failed her and was an uncaring, unloving, self-absorbed grandson. His distortions of the actual events laid the foundation for his self-downing and debilitating guilt.

Accept Your Fallibility and Erase the Distortions

The quote by Albert Ellis that opened this chapter— *To err proves human; to forgive leaves you sane and realistic*—is not only rational but very instructive. Accepting your less-than-perfect nature as a human being will position you to accept your errors and decide if these are things you wish to address and amend. Guilt and shame are not needed for such a decision and growth.

The distorted, faulty thinking that results in our shame and guilt can be reformulated. It will not be easy, but with persistence, you can reformulate your thinking in a way that helps you accept your fallibility while engaging in actions that move you in the direction you desire.

How can you begin? Let's try two different approaches to attacking shame and guilt.

PLAN A: JOURNALING

Using your thought journal, identify and describe a situation or an event associated with your sense of guilt or shame. Next, identify and list your thoughts about your actions, about you as a person, that are associated with that event, those actions. As you revisit these thoughts, challenge them using the following questions.

1. Is what you did or failed to do some violation of an absolute law, an absolute should that applies to all, or is it merely something you (and perhaps others) see as undesirable?

2. Is what you did or failed to do evidence that you are exceptional and uniquely flawed? Unacceptable? Wretched? Or is this something that others may do or fail to do?

3. What are the real, factual consequences of your actions or inactions? Are they survivable? Can they be reversed or at least modified? Can you and those involved move on?

4. Is it possible for you to learn from this experience? Could you, if you choose, grow as a result of this experience?

5. Does what you did (or failed to do) negate any of your other positive characteristics, attributes, behaviors?

Using your responses to each of the above, reformulate your assessment, your interpretation of your actions and the events associated with your guilt/shame. Does this view more accurately reflect the facts of the situation and position you to take responsibility for your actions (or inactions) and decide if you would like to act differently in similar future situations? If so—it would appear this new perspective is much more effective and supportive of your emotional well-being.

PLAN B: SHAME ATTACK

One way to attack our hypersensitivity to the judgments of others and the sense of shame that may result when we experience disapproval is to merely engage in something that is entirely ridiculous or outside of "normal" social protocol without offering an explanation to buffer the reaction. The objective of this exercise is to expose you to the criticism of others. Do something that others would most likely think is ridiculous. Engage in an activity where others will look at you strangely and maybe even snicker or pass comments.

Since the goal is to make you socially uncomfortable and invite critical glances or comments from others, select something that is indeed outside of your comfort zone. The rule of thumb is—if you feel the shame or discomfort when something comes to mind, it is probably an opportunity to consider the act as a potentially worthwhile shame and discomfort attack. Just remember, only do it if it is not hurting anyone, it is not illegal, and it is not against your long-term goals. Some ideas include:

1. Sing at a restaurant or bar karaoke night.
2. Go out with clothing that you like but which may not be something a person your age, position, or gender would typically wear.
3. Ask a question that others may consider "stupid,"

but you really don't know the answer and would like to.

4. Tell a joke to an audience who would be surprised by your presentation.
5. Walk down the street or in the aisle of a store and sing a song aloud.
6. While at a casual social lunch, provide a toast or blessing (if inclined).
7. When in an elevator or standing in a line, introduce yourself to a stranger.
8. When in an elevator or standing in a line, compliment a stranger on a specific physical characteristic, an item of clothing, or even perfume/cologne.

In performing these acts, you will most likely notice one of two things. First, it is very likely that others will either not notice or not care about your actions. Secondly, even when others do notice and pass judgment (by a look or comment), nothing horrible really happens. You move on as do they.

If, however, you encounter another person who responds to your actions with negative judgment and evaluation, ask yourself the following:

- What does it mean that this person is passing judgment on me and what I just did?
- How does their judgment change the person I am?
- How does their judgment significantly impact my life and interfere with my ability to enjoy my life?

- How did this act change my value as a human being?

Yes, others may look at what you did and pass judgment. That is their right. However, their opinion does not make you any different than what you are. There is not cause for shame. Remind yourself that if you are feeling shame, it is you creating your own shame. It is you buying into their judgment of YOU as a bad or unacceptable person that is causing your shame. Stop such "crazy" thinking, and you will find that you live life much more freely and authentically.

CHAPTER 7

From Needing Approval to Merely Desiring It

*If you just set out to be liked, you would be
prepared to compromise
on anything at any time and would
achieve nothing.*

—Margaret Thatcher

I DID A quick search of song lyrics with the phrase "I need your love." The results? Lyrics.com reported 250,624 lyrics, 115 artists, and 100 albums matching my search phrase. Now, don't get me wrong. I like music and will accept that the term "need" may be being used with literary license. But sadly, many individuals truly believe that they *need* to be accepted, if not outright loved, by others. For people driven to gain approval from others, what might be a mere desire or wish has become an all-encompassing need. With this as their self-created reality, they may find themselves engaging in behaviors that not only attempt to win approval at any cost but in the process undermine their emotional well-being. The need to continually gain approval can become a life quest. It is a quest that at one moment can provide an artificial high and the next plummet one into despair.

This roller-coaster experience was illustrated by one of my college-aged clients who described herself as the "queen of selfies." The problem wasn't that she engaged in taking and posting pictures of herself in various locations and situations on social media; the problem was that she would allow the evaluative comments from those on social media to control her emotional ups and downs.

As she explained, she "enjoyed" taking pictures of herself wearing a new outfit, or eating at an upscale restaurant, or posing at various locations. She admitted, however, that she felt as if she had to post her pictures on social media. Once having posted the latest selfie, she found herself obsessively checking on all reactions and comments to her posting. Reviews that were complimentary seemed to skyrocket her self-evaluation. Conversely, those that were negative and critical seemed to drive her in the dumps.

She pointed to positive comments that would seem to make her feel great, such as: "You're hot!" "Great hair," "It must be great to be you!" In listening to her description of these comments, it became clear that she did not simply see them as nice compliments, but rather as essential evidence in proving her worth and value. Given this distorted view of the importance, the need for positive evaluation, it was not surprising to find that negative comments truly rocked her sense of self and self-worth. Her dire need to pursue affirmation made her vulnerable to falling into despair when such feedback was not received. Seeing comments such as "I can't believe you went out in public with that dress" or "Your hair looks like a rat's nest" not only tore her down but created even a greater need to gain approval from someone, anyone…for any reason.

Over time, she began to focus only on the negative comments, literally filtering out any positives, and as a result, she fell into a state of despair and depression. With her selective collection of negative comments as her reference point, she concluded that no one liked her or would ever like her since she was so unappealing.

The Cost of Needing Approval

When your desire for approval elevates to the level of *a need*, you place yourself in a position where you will experience not just pain and sadness but devastation at the hands of rejection. Operating from a position of needing approval makes you vulnerable to the manipulation of others. Such a desperate need for another's approval empowers them to hold out this approval as a way of manipulation. This is perhaps most clearly illustrated by an individual who remains in a long-standing, abusive relationship.

One of my clients came to therapy at the "demand" of

her sister. The client, as the story unfolded, had been in a psychologically abusive marriage for the past eleven years. Her family and friends agreed that the relationship was an unhealthy one, but all attempts at encouraging the couple, or my client by herself, to seek help went unheeded. She now came to therapy, not with a goal of making decisions about her abusive relationship, but rather to find ways that she "could be a better wife."

She noted that her husband had never physically abused her and that his anger was justified. She dismissed his negative comments that attacked her appearance, her intelligence, her housekeeping, as being justified. "Look at me, I am a fat pig, and I do nothing around the house; it looks like a pigsty." While it was clear that this barrage of negative comments had driven my client into a state of depression, even that state of depression was now viewed by my client as more justification for the husband's criticism.

The question could be asked—given the abuse why doesn't she just leave? The answer to that question becomes clear once we appreciate that from her perspective the negative comments were a small price to pay for those times when he would convey approval and acceptance. For this client, and others in similar situations, her value as a person was dependent on achieving the approval from her husband, and she was willing to endure whatever it took to experience those moments of acceptance. She provided multiple justifications for his behavior, stating things such as: "He's a good guy. I love him, and he can be nice to me. I just have to stop screwing up and making him mad. I know I can do better..."

When experienced as an essential life need, this desire for approval positions a person to be willing to "pay"' with their time, their interests, their energy, so that they can get that sign of approval. The concern about doing something wrong or in some way eliciting rejection rather than approval can even result in the situation where an individual will have difficulty in making decisions, or at least will refrain from expressing his decision.

For someone so dependent upon the approval of others, the risk of sharing her opinion or expressing her needs, in the absence of knowing what the other will affirm, becomes overwhelming. After all, without knowing what one needs to express or select that in turn would be pleasing to the other, one risks rejection—and rejection for one needing approval is intolerable.

But the cost of needing approval doesn't stop there.

For the person who has a desperate need for approval, there is never enough positive feedback or affirmation and approval to satisfy the need that has been created. Given this unquenchable need for approval, the person becomes obsessed with receiving positive feedback and evidence of acceptability. Such "neediness" can destroy the very relationship they so desperately need. This was the case for one college senior who was having a tough time in her current relationship. As she explained, the relationship, which started so positively, had now become a major burden, or as she stated, a real "albatross" around her neck. She stated that they had been dating for about three months when he started to act in very "possessive" ways. He was constantly checking up on her, calling her and asking where she was, who she was with, and what she was doing. In addition to this type of behavior, he began to ask for evidence that she still cared for him constantly. His increasing neediness was truly destroying the relationship. "He's killing me with his neediness. He is constantly up my butt checking to see if I love him, if everything is okay with our relationship. He must ask me a thousand times a day if I still find him attractive, and it goes on and on and on. He's killing me; I am suffocating!"

The potential for a mutually rewarding and affirming relationship appeared to have existed in this situation; the problem was my client's counterpart didn't merely want a relationship, but desperately NEEDED one. It was this desperate need for acceptance that resulted in his actions, which ultimately destroyed the very thing he wanted.

Why So Needy?

While there is no one explanation for the development of such a high need for approval, theories about human development often suggest that children's sense of self-worth emerges from an internalization of the views of significant others. The problem can occur when a child develops in an environment where there is only "conditional valuing." In this environment, the experience of receiving praise and affirmation or rejection is a function of how the child looks or behaves. In these situations getting an

"A" or making a hit on the baseball team were not merely accomplishments to celebrate but were the ticket needed to gain parental approval and even love. It was in meeting the standards of others that these individuals felt worth and value. Sadly, it was not the child who was valued but the conditions surrounding that child.

Having developed this perspective on the value, the need for other's approval, these individuals will approach social interactions and relationships willing to act and present in ways that increase the chances of receiving approval.

Cognitive Distortions Supporting an Unhealthy Need for Approval

Experiencing affirmation and approval from others can be nice. There are times when seeking and receiving such approval is quite functional. This would undoubtedly be the case when we are trying to impress our employer in hopes of gaining some promotion. However, when the drive for approval is resulting in self-harming decisions, the mediating cognitive distortions need to be attacked and reformulated. The following is a sampling of cognitive distortions that if employed can support an unhealthy need for approval.

MAGNIFICATION:

Simply put, magnification is taking an event or experience, including the experience of approval or rejection, and exaggerating its value out of proportion. While being liked by another and avoiding rejection may be desirable, this approval *is not* essential to your survival, nor is it essential to your happiness or emotional well-being. For those engaging magnification in the processing of an experience of acceptance or rejection, the merely desirable becomes essential. Believing, truly believing, that "I couldn't live without you" is neither factual nor is it at all functional.

Those who have elevated a desire for acceptance and approval to a dire need will do well to challenge this cognitive error of magnification. It is crucial to rein in any desperate need for approval. Your emotional well-being is best served when you need to see the desire for approval as it is, a simple desire, a wish, or a want, and *not* a necessity. Seeing approval as a preference will allow you to enjoy it when it is received and merely be disappointed when it is not.

Empowering Others

One significant error an approval seeker often makes is to view another's reactions and evaluations as valid assessments of their worth. Perhaps you know someone who takes to heart the negative comments of others. A comment such as "you are so dumb," when tied to a person making a simple mistake, becomes destructive when the recipient buys into that label, that evaluation, and believes that the evaluator has the ability to accurately and definitively pass such judgment.

The idea is not to completely dismiss the opinions, the judgments, the evaluations of others in your life. Their comments might be instructive. They may be inviting you to consider some relevant information that you were not aware of and, in the process, identify areas of your life that are ripe for development. However, it is essential to remember that whether another's reactions are approving or rejecting in nature, these reactions, these judgments are only a reflection of that person's very limited and subjective assessment of your behavior, your performance, or your characteristics. Their evaluations, no matter how they are framed or labeled—cannot be nor ever will be a VALID ASSESSMENT OF YOU AS A PERSON.

It is true that other people, like you, have every right to their opinion of these things. It is only their opinion, their very personal and subjective opinion, based on insufficient information and assessed with a standard that is indeed subjective. Their opinions are not absolute truths for all to embrace. To believe another person has the authority to declare you or me as acceptable or reject-able is providing them with power that they do not possess.

You may have made a mistake, so it may be helpful to consider their evaluation; it may be accurate and valid when applied to that one situation, that one event or action. However, the fact that you made a mistake or even multiple mistakes is not evidence supporting an assessment of you as being a dumb, unacceptable person.

Take a moment and review your own experiences of rejection. It might help to write the event out. Where was it? Who was the evaluator(s)? What is the basis for the evaluation and the resulting rejection?

Without knowing your experience or how you may have answered each of the above questions, I believe that regardless of the situation, it was not and never could have been a rejection of you, the person. This situation, like all that you have experienced where another expressed their approval or disapproval, was an experience of someone else's subjective opinion about some condition or characteristic of you (e.g., your clothes, your comment, your behavior, your values, etc.) occurring at some limited time in your life. Hopefully, you know that and even remembered that at the time of this rejection. Remembering this and stubbornly refusing to give another the power of approval of you as a human being will help you defeat any unhealthy, dire need for approval.

MUSTERBATING

Albert Ellis, the father of rational emotive therapy, coined the term "musterbating" to describe the phenomenon whereby people live by a set of absolute and unrealistic demands they place on themselves, others, and the world. It is often the engagement in such "musterbating" thinking that positions a person to move from merely desiring approval to now believing that it is essential to his well-being and thus MUST be achieved. Operating with this belief positions the person to not only view the reception of approval a must but that he MUST be, act, look, a certain way so that he can achieve the affirmation so desperately needed. I remember one client who explained her decision to engage with numerous sexual partners as simply: "...something I have to do, they expect it, and if I don't, they won't want to hang with me."

For this client, the need to receive some sign of approvability, even if approvability was conditional and tied to actions that she would rather have not performed, led her to view her behavior as simply the expected price for acceptance, something that she had to (must) do. As suggested in this case, believing that "others must like, if not love, me" places one in a position of doing whatever is necessary to gain evidence of that liking, that approval.

It is essential for one's emotional well-being to understand and embrace the fact that there are no MUSTS or SHOULDS, merely wishes and wants. Approaching the desire to be accepted and receive approval as a want, a wish, a desire, rather than a life-essential must will help you be merely disappointed when such approval is not received, rather than devastated. Non-approval is genuinely not the end of the world, nor the need for the destruction of your emotional well-being.

AWFULIZING (CATASTROPHIZING)

Perhaps we could consider awfulizing as an extension of magnification as applied to negative outcomes. With awfulizing or catastrophizing an individual sees an undesirable or disappointing event as absolutely intolerable and unbearable.

It follows that for people who genuinely hold the belief that another's approval is ESSENTIAL to their happiness and well-being, encountering rejection or times of failing to gain that approval will be viewed and consequentially felt like intolerable CATASTROPHES.

To defeat the "crazies" of awfulizing and its negative impact on your emotional well-being, you must step back and engage in a significant reality check. When in the grips of catastrophic thinking, you need to review the situation as objectively as possible and identify the real, concrete consequences of failing to achieve approval at this time and within this context. There may be real consequences to rejection. These consequences may be unsettling and even somewhat inconvenient, but these consequences, even when they cannot be changed, are tolerable, and certainly not unbearable catastrophes.

When applied to a dire need for approval, the ability to recognize and reject catastrophic thinking will help you embrace rejection as a bump in the road, not the end of your happiness. Resisting catastrophic thinking will help you move the gaining of approval to the realm of the desirable and out of the world of essential. Being able to decatastrophize rejection will position you to make decisions that will engage you in life and support your emotional well-being.

Wanting, Not Needing, Approval

The process of developing and maintaining emotional well-being starts with your ability to face disapproval and rejection in a healthy and useful way. Each of the following practices can help you build and maintain a healthy perspective, one desiring approval while vigorously resisting needing approval.

GET OUT THE THOUGHT JOURNAL

There is real value to the process of writing down your negative thoughts and beliefs about any experience with disapproval or rejection. Placing your interpretation of the event down on paper invites you to review the situation and your interpretation with a more objective eye. As you revisit the circumstance or situation of felt rejection, use the following questions to challenge your interpretation, your perspective, and give shape to a new more rational view.

- What real, concrete consequences will I experience as a result of failing to receive approval in this context?
- How, precisely, will these consequences impact my life, my happiness, and for how long?
- Do I honestly need this approval to make my life enjoyable? Or more simply put, if I fail to gain approval at any one point, does that in any way

honestly take away the other joys in my life? Will my favorite ice cream no longer taste good because of this rejection?

- How does the fact that I want—maybe even desperately want—approval serve as evidence that another person must give it to me? Do they genuinely have the ability, the power, to proclaim to the world that I am an approvable human being?

- When I receive this desired approval, what is it that they are approving? Me? Something I did or said? A condition about me?

- Okay—so the approval, the affirmation, is not forthcoming, or more directly, I am experiencing rejection. So what? What happens when I step back and investigate how "bad" it is to receive criticism, rejection, or disapproval? Is my life over?

REPLACE OTHER-ACCEPTANCE WITH SELF-ACCEPTANCE

Perhaps one of the best antidotes to the unhealthy need for approval is to develop a balanced, accurate view of you and with it an unconditional sense of self-acceptance (see chapter 8). When you recognize your strengths and talents, as well as own your own defined flaws or areas of potential growth, you will free yourself from an unhealthy need for another's affirmation or approval. You won't need me to tell you are good at this or that; you will know it. You won't be surprised by my criticism in that you will have already identified this condition and accepted it or rejected it as a target to be addressed or will be surprised by the feedback and be open to consider its value.

Developing a philosophy and approach to life that shifts the focus from "other approval" to "self-approval" is not easy. The following are reminders of steps to be taken as you continue to develop just such a shift in philosophy and in so doing increase your emotional happiness and well-being.

Shifting the Focus from "Other" to "Self" Approval

While you are not likely able to control the assessment of others, you can control the emotional impact such assessment has on you. The process starts by embracing each of the following directives and practicing them frequently so that they become part of your approach to life.

1. ***Give Up on People Pleasing***: Give yourself permission to do and say what works for you. This doesn't mean to stop caring about the impact of your words or actions, nor does it mean that you should now be inconsiderate of others' wishes and wants. It merely means STOP putting YOU on hold until another gives you permission. It may be an act as simple as saying no or yes to a second helping at dinner. Maybe your host will take offense at your refusal or, on the other hand, feel that you are a bit pushy asking for more. That would be a shame, for

them. Your intent is neither to offend nor elicit approval; it is merely an effort to address your hunger needs. In this case, the encounter is one of dining, not of pleasing. Remember this as applied in all your encounters. Is it about meeting your legitimate needs, or an exercise in people pleasing?

2. *Give Up the Illusion of Power*: Remind yourself that you DO NOT have the power to make other people happy or upset. While it is true you may be able to influence their opinion some of the time, you can't control it. Yes, your dinner host may be a tad bit disappointed that you refused the second helping, but that is his issue, not yours. You certainly have the freedom to be concerned about his dismay and perhaps choose to offer both a compliment and an explanation as to your current state of fullness. However, for you to maintain your emotional well-being, you need to remember that his happiness or dismay is not your responsibility or within your power.

3. *Accept that Being True to Self Can Come with Costs*: Standing up for what you believe can sometimes mean standing alone. Saying no when others say yes, or saying yes when others remain silent, can be difficult. Resisting group or peer pressure can be difficult. Being out of step with others may make it difficult to receive evidence of these others' affirmation and approval but can be what is needed if in service of your needs. While being

true to yourself can be hard at any one moment, it is essential to your long-term health and emotional well-being to remain true to you.

4. *Find Growth in Criticism*: Doing your own thing and providing your own self-approval does not mean you should be impervious to feedback, be that positive or negative. There can be value and growth opportunities in considering the feedback you receive. For such feedback to be of value you need to: (a) remember it is a reflection of another's subjective view and values; (b) understand that it is feedback tied to specific conditions about you, not you as a person; and (c) attempt to view the input as objectively as possible. It is important to remember that observations, opinions, and perspectives shared by others may help you with your ongoing development, but only if it is a direction you choose to go.

CHAPTER 8

Less Than a Perfect Ten (Accepting Yourself As You Are)

I was once afraid of people saying "Who does she think she is?"
Now I have the courage to stand and say "This is who I am."

—Oprah Winfrey

I ATTENDED A college graduation where the keynote speaker was an 85-year-old woman of Navajo descent. Before presenting her commencement speech, she thanked everyone for their kindness but noted that she found some of the comments quite curious. She expressed some confusion over a comment that many people made when meeting her: "Wow, you don't look eighty-five." The comments were meant to be complimentary of her youthful appearance. She found the comment curious because as she noted: "This is how eighty-five looks on me." It would appear that for her a youthful appearance, unblemished skin, and minimal wrinkles were nothing to be celebrated; they were just artifacts of being who she was. She accepted herself as she was, but sadly this is not true for all of us.

Through the wonders of modern science, we can now have plump lips, wrinkle-less brows, enhanced body parts, regrown hair, and so many more "improvements." The quest for the perfect ten has led to a multibillion-dollar industry in cosmetics and cosmetic surgery. I am not suggesting that there is anything intrinsically wrong with improving (in your eyes) your appearance. However, when perfection, be it in appearance or performance, becomes your absolute criterion for self-acceptance, we have a problem.

Seek Healthy Self-Acceptance

Let's start with the obvious. Neither you nor anyone else is, or will ever be, perfect. We are works in progress, and like all works in progress, we can use a little refinement, some fine-tuning or polishing. However, while losing pounds, ridding yourself of wrinkles, or even gaining advancement in your career may have real benefits—none of these "achievements" or changes makes you more valuable as a human being. Don't buy that statement? Well, let's do a little "mind experiment."

I want you to pretend you bought a new outfit. It fits well, and it is the color you love. When you look at yourself, you are pleased with the way it all comes together. Great. Do the new style and appearance make you a better, more valuable human being? Okay, maybe that was too easy. How about fixing that area of your body with which you are less than pleased? Would bigger muscles, less body fat, and a smoother, more youthful appearance make you a better, more valued person? Assuming you said no to both of those questions, can you genuinely identify anything about you that if you made perfect would significantly increase your value as a human being?

It is in embracing the fact of your imperfection, while at the same time working to grow and improve in ways you desire, that you will be able to experience *real, healthy self-acceptance*. Healthy self-acceptance is founded upon a balanced, accurate view of you. It is the recognition of your strengths and talents as well as owning your self-defined flaws or areas of potential growth.

Healthy self-acceptance is one that reflects an understanding that what you or others identify as your talents or strengths do not make you anything more than you are. Similarly, regardless of the laundry list of "flaws" you or another could generate, it is important to remember that this list depicts nothing more than the fact that you, like everyone else, are human. To be perfectly human is to be imperfect.

Accepting this will help you resist the temptation to generalize from your evaluation of a this or a that, to labeling and assessment of your entire "self." Look in the mirror. See that muscle? Doesn't it make you special? No. Okay, so how about that wrinkle or little extra pouch of fat—do they make you unacceptable? Nope. These characteristics make you *you*, and that in and of itself is good enough reason to feel valued.

I once had a client who was stuck in the perfection quagmire. She was continually finding and amplifying her limitations, especially those concerning her body and physical appearance. As an exercise, I invited her to gather some old pictures of herself. I asked her to search for photos that reflected various times of her development, from birth (if she could find one), through early childhood, adolescence, young adulthood, to the most recent ones she had. In our session, she shared the photos.

Now, before I had a chance to look at them, she began to apologize and make self-demeaning comments in regard to her most recent pictures, stating: "These are not good." "I know I've gained weight, but these couple from my vacation last year make me look like a moose." "I am disgusting-looking in these beach pictures."

As I began looking at each picture, I would ask the same type of questions. Looking at a baby picture, one of about eight months of age, I asked: "Tell me about how old you were in this picture and what one physical characteristic or attribute displayed is in your opinion attractive or cute." After she responded to this question, I then asked her, "Again, looking at this picture, what one physical characteristic or attribute being displayed is something you find appalling and wish you could change?"

For each of the "pre-now" pictures, I asked the same two questions and each time deliberately used the word "appalling" in the second question. To my surprise, she challenged my use of the term. She was able to identify things in each of these pictures that she felt were less than ideal. For example, she noted that at eight months old she had a somewhat "fat baby face" and as a pre-teen, she had "spaced teeth," and later as a teen, acne. Each of these characteristics she labeled as less than perfect but was quick to dismiss my term "appalling," replacing it with "less than ideal." As we discussed the good, the bad, and the ugly, at least as she perceived it, I asked two more questions about these pictures. "What happened to the less-than-ideal trait?" For example, what happened to the plump baby face or spaced teeth or acne? It was easy for her to recognize not only the transient nature of these conditions but the developmental appropriateness. Babies often have chubby cheeks, some pre-teens benefit from braces, and acne is a common experience during the hormonal period of adolescence. As I flipped back through these early pictures, I asked her to "Tell me which of the individuals portrayed in these various pictures had the most value and was most deserving of love?" As you might suspect, she suggested that was a dumb question, and I agreed.

We continued this process of reviewing and evaluating the most recent vacation pictures. In reviewing the pictures in light of the questions, she came to the following conclusions. First, what she valued concerning her body and physical makeup changes over time. Secondly, the criteria for her evaluation of her physical characteristics, either positive or negative, were utterly subjective. Finally, and perhaps most importantly, she noted that regardless of the physical attributes, the person portrayed was just as valuable and loveable as the eight-month-old baby.

With this little exercise, she began to see and embrace the fact that she has always possessed traits or characteristics that she subjectively valued and others that she viewed negatively. But most importantly she realized that none of these characteristics changed the fact that she was a person deserving of self-acceptance.

Self-Acceptance Is NOT Resignation

Self-acceptance is merely the process of embracing our whole self, including what we deem the good, the bad, and the ugly. Accepting yourself as you are at any moment in time, imperfections and all, does not mean that you are self-satisfied. Self-acceptance does not suggest that you should be in total resignation of the conditions of your life or your circumstances.

I can remember one of my clients somewhat sarcastically challenging me by saying, "Oh, good, I am self-accepting. I don't have to change." My response was "Yep, actually, you never did have to change." It is not a matter of "have to" but rather "want to."

Nothing being suggested here is meant to imply that

with self-acceptance one should fall into a state of complacency. The ability to accept yourself as you are at this point in time allows you to engage in efforts, if you so choose, to move in directions that you see as desirable. Being free of self-evaluation allows you to be critical of those aspects of your life and yourself that you find less than optimal while resisting the tendency to generalize and judge your total person as less than optimal. Further, with self-acceptance, you will realize there is nothing that needs to be done that will make you more acceptable. You are acceptable by the very fact of being you.

Self-Acceptance and Personal Growth

As noted, self-acceptance does not equate with self-complacency. With self-acceptance as a foundation, you can review your self-defined rough spots, your challenges, and your areas of desired improvement without the pressure of believing that improvement or rectification is essential to gaining personal worth and acceptability. Being free to view your life, yourself, in the absence of a need to defend your value as a person allows you to take a critical look at yourself and decide if there is something that you would like to change

Accepting the reality of you at this point is empowering. Freeing yourself from self-imposed embarrassment or shame because of your holiday binging and the resulting increase in your waist size is an important step in deciding if exercising and dieting are something you wish to pursue. But taking steps for "self-improvement" cannot occur if rather than simply seeing extra pounds on the scale, you see evidence of you being "fat," "ugly," "disgusting," or some other negative valuing of self.

With self-acceptance, we are free to celebrate and enjoy our talents and accomplishments while at the same time embracing, without self-berating, our weaknesses, limitations, or even our failures.

Becoming Self-Accepting

When discussing this issue of self-acceptance with one of my clients, I was challenged with the question: "If self-acceptance is simply embracing the fact that as a human being I am imperfect and that's the way it is supposed to be, then why is it so damn difficult to buy in to that?"

Why is it so damn difficult to truly embrace the fact that we are acceptable as less-than-perfect beings? That is a great question, and the answer is perhaps too simple.

Our difficulty in accepting and working with this truth is that we have been taught to value self "conditionally." For many individuals, personal worth and value are dependent upon having a model's physique, the latest clothes, the luxury car, and the desired address. For too many individuals these conditions are needed and used as evidence that they are valuable and worthwhile.

Buying into a standard of conditional worth fosters the development of specific cognitive distortions that blind us to the reality of self-acceptance. While numerous forms of cognitive distortions can contribute to a client's failure to be self-accepting, two—All-or-None Thinking and Generalizations/Labeling—appear particularly detrimental to full, unconditional, and healthy acceptance of self.

ALL-OR-NONE THINKING

If there were a prescription for creating and maintaining non-self-acceptance, it would be to view everything you do in absolute terms. See yourself as either a success or a failure. Don't allow for any middle ground. The rule is simple: be perfect or be unacceptable.

Those who exhibit perfectionistic tendency often operate from an "all or none" type of thinking. When assessing their performance, individuals employing all-or-none thinking see things as totally good or bad. There are no shades of gray with this type of thinking. A single mistake or error is not merely a mistake or error; it is evidence of failing and being a failure. This type of thinking was presented in full form by one of my clients, whom I will call Carlos.

Carlos shared his history, one that gave much evidence of this tendency to be extremely hard on himself. All throughout his teen years, he would berate himself for his appearance, especially his weight. He would be hypercritical about his limited athletic abilities, and most significantly down himself for what he felt was his lack of interpersonal skills and attractiveness to the opposite sex. While it was clear that he had numerous successes in each of these arenas, his perception was that unless it was "perfect," it was a "perfect failure."

During one of our sessions, he told me about his decision to drop out of graduate school. Carlos was going through a graduate program in teacher education and had just received his first field supervision evaluation. He shared the review with me, and it was evident that on the eight elements assessed, he was judged as competent in all eight areas. The commentary pointed to his enthusiasm, his understanding of the material presented, and his apparent level of preparation. For areas of growth that he was invited to consider, the evaluator noted: *Carlos, as with any beginning teacher you tend to be more focused on doing your plan than teaching the students. It will help when you can relax and adjust your plan on the go, according to the students' responses to what you are doing. This flexibility will come, and you are off to a good start.*

While it appeared to me that the evaluation was very supportive, Carlos was quick to point at the evaluator's comment regarding being overly focused on delivering his lesson plan, and he responded: "Look at this. I blew it. Look at this. I was not focused on teaching the students. How could I ever be a teacher? I need to go back to working at the insurance agency. Who will trust me with their children?"

Carlos processed the evaluation through the distorted lens of all-or-nothing thinking. As such, he negated or at least ignored all of the supportive comments and now only focused on the one critical observation that for him was evidence not just of an area for growth, but evidence of total failure. For Carlos, anything less than 100 percent perfect translated into 100 percent failure.

All-or-none thinking can disrupt attempts to change any behavior, from efforts to lose weight, to stop smoking, or to improve job-related skills. If an individual approaches these tasks with a standard of perfection, one minor slip-up is enough to derail all efforts, since from this perspective anything short of 100 percent might as well be 0 percent.

There is nothing wrong or dysfunctional about being critical of your less-than-perfect performance. To be of use, however, such a critical evaluation needs to include all the data involved in the particular situation. Including all the data before concluding will help you defend again the error of all-or-none thinking, which would direct you to employ one element, one data point, to color the entire situation. Perhaps you did binge over the weekend, but wasn't it true you stuck to your diet the week before? With a more objective and expansive view of the good, the less-than-good, and the in-betweens, you will be positioned to set meaningful goals and plans for growth while being accepting of yourself as you are at this point.

GENERALIZATION AND LABELING

Generalization is a cognitive error in which you take one event, experience, or characteristic and spread your generalization to all events, experiences, or characteristic.

With generalization, you use the reality of failing this exam and then conclude that you will fail the course and even fail out of school.

When generalizations occur and are applied to self, it is not unusual to find that the individual shifts from assessing the specific area of concern to "labeling" themselves as failures, rotten, stupid, etc. The sequence would go from, "I made a mistake" to "I screw up everything (generalization)" and finally, to "I'm such a loser" (labeling). Such declaration of being "totally bad," "worthless," "a loser," "a waste," etc. undermines any hope of unconditional self-acceptance.

Returning to my client, Carlos, it was clear that he held unrealistic perfectionistic standards in judging his performance. Further, taking his less-than-perfect performance, he generalized and concluded that he could no longer do anything related to teaching and that he needed to find less challenging work. With this as his perspective on the event and his performance, he quickly transitioned away from his behavior to the labeling of himself, stating: "I am such a loser, I could never be trusted with a child's future." This belief that he was a "loser" with no future resulted in his experience of depression.

Combating the cognitive distortions of generalization and labeling will require that you shift your assessments from a focus on your total "self" to an objective, yet critical view of your actions. Quite often just gaining a more objective view of the situation will help reduce the tendency to engage in overgeneralization and labeling. Another strategy to help defeat any inclination to engage in over-generalization and labeling is to challenge your perspective by reflecting on questions such as the following.:

- Do you always perform (e.g., fail a test) that way?
- Are there times when you have acted in the way you desired (i.e., been successful)?
- Would you apply this same standard to a friend or a loved one and similarly label them (i.e., falling short once means that they are losers and unacceptable)?

The data provided by responding to each of the above questions will position you to gain a healthy, useful perspective on your experience. So for the person falling into a hopeless feeling about his chances to succeed in college after failing one test, the questions may stimulate a response such as: "Yes, I failed this test. Yes, I am having a hard time in this class. I've passed my labs and the first two tests. I have a final and a paper coming up, so I have an opportunity to improve my grade. I certainly would not think my girlfriend was a loser for failing one test—in fact, I would encourage her to learn what she did wrong so that she could do better on the next." This perspective will not only help him defend against the use of generalization and labeling to process the experience but position him for unconditional self-acceptance, even while he plans on taking steps to improve his test performance and overall grades in that class.

A Self-Accepting Perspective

As you move toward unconditional self-acceptance, it is helpful to not only be on guard against employing the "crazies" of "all or none" thinking and "generalization/ labeling" but also develop a healthier, more realistic self-accepting perspective. It is helpful to remember and embrace the following "truisms."

1. It is true you will mess up. We will make mistakes.
2. While errors can have consequences, some quite negative, the truth of the matter is that you did not set out to make a mistake. You did the best you possibly could have done, given the actual circumstances of that moment.
3. You don't need to feel good about falling short of goals, but you need to embrace the reality that not only did you do your best, but if you can shed the negatively biased self-referencing and accept yourself as you are, then perhaps you can learn from these failings.

The following exercise invites you to challenge your tendency to engage in conditional valuing.

Moving Away From Conditional Valuing

Directions: In the table below, identify (in column A) one particular strength, talent, or valued capability that you have demonstrated. Now, for each of the areas listed below, identify (in column B) one specific error, mistake, weakness, or challenge that you have exhibited. After doing these two steps, consider the questions that follow.

Areas/Domains	Column A: Strength, Talent, or Valued Characteristic	Column B: Evidence of Error, Mistake, Shortcoming
Interpersonal relationships		
School or job performance		
Self-care		
Personal responsibilities		
Intellectual and social-emotional characteristics		

Given what you listed in the table, consider each of the following.

- Does anything listed in column B (a mistake, a failure, a criticism, a fault or weakness) take away anything listed in column A?
- What one thing in column B justifies labelling your total self as a failure, a weak person, incompetent, worthless, or any negative label?
- If you were to argue against your unconditional self-acceptance, what part of the data listed would you use as evidence? How would you deal with the non-supportive data? Would you use the same rationale and criteria to judge others in your life?

While there may be value in judging your actions, primarily as they serve or fail to serve your goals and purposes, employing any negative assessment of your behavior as criteria for assigning worth to your total self is not only "crazy" but will undermine your emotional well-being. Rejecting conditional valuing and worth is essential if we are to maintain our psychological health and emotional well-being.

CHAPTER 9

Depression: Well Beyond Sadness

As if I am a prisoner of an overwhelming sense of hopelessness and helplessness.
—Anonymous

THE DESCRIPTION OF depression that opens this chapter was one offered to me by one of my clients as he attempted to explain his experience with depression. While most of us have had moments, even extended periods of sadness in our life, if you have experienced depression, you know that this is something that goes well beyond what most of us know as sadness.

When sad you may decide to withdraw from contact with others. When sad you may find that you often cry and may, at least in the short term, lose your desire to engage in those activities that you previously enjoyed. To some degree, the same is true for one who is depressed. But depression is not simply a greater quantity of sadness.

The difference between sadness and depression is not one merely of degree. Depression is off the continuum of sadness and reflects a qualitatively unique and devastating experience. One significant difference and singularly devastating characteristic of depression is that it is most often accompanied by the belief that things are completely hopeless, that there is no end in sight, and that it is a condition for which you are helpless. This type of thinking may lead those with depression to consider death, even suicide, as their only way out.

Cognitive Errors and Depression

It is entirely possible that when depressed you can identify a real-world event that you have associated with the creation of your depression. Perhaps you recently experienced a significant loss in your life—be that of a loved one, a job, even one of your capabilities. While feelings of sadness often accompany significant loss, that sadness can transform into depression when the events are filtered through beliefs (i.e., cognitive distortions) that transform that experience from one of pain and sorrow to one that is hopeless and unbearable.

When it comes to depression, cognitive distortions such as catastrophizing, overgeneralization, and selective abstraction often appear to be operating.

Catastrophic Thinking and Depression

Life can present some very severe challenges. Illness,

significant financial setbacks, family tragedies, and loss of loved ones are part of life and can have a significant impact on those experiencing such events. Even with the significance of these events and the real consequences they pose, we can process these occurrences in such a way as to exaggerate and maximize their negativity to the point of defining them and experiencing them as overwhelming crises. Often those suffering from depression are exaggerating the actual events and consequences they have encountered and thus catastrophizing a perspective of their life as one in which they are helpless, and all is hopeless.

Perhaps you are familiar with the actor Christopher Reeve. Here was a young man, age forty-two, married with children and a very successful acting career. Reeve had a horse-riding accident and, as a result, suffered fractures to his top two vertebrae, considered the most serious of cervical injuries, damaging his spinal cord. This was indeed a severe situation. It imposed real challenges, threats, and limitations on his life.

Here was a man who stared as Superman in the movies and now found himself paralyzed and needing assistance to breathe. But even in this situation, where his control over much of his physical functioning had been taken away, the emotional impact of this loss remained within his power. As he noted: "Once you choose hope, anything's possible."

In reviewing his life following the accident, it appears that he chose to see his life as it was, stubbornly refusing to filter his many challenges through cognitive distortions that would create the hopeless, helpless sense of depression. While I don't pretend to know the psychological struggle he confronted or the thoughts he may have had, I do know that the choices he made in the face of this situation would not have occurred if he believed that it was hopeless and that he was helpless and worthless. Christopher Reeve did not surrender. He did not catastrophize, making the situation worse than it was. He understood that there were now many things he could no longer do. At the same time, however, he knew there were things in his life he could still enjoy and opportunities to find meaning and value. True, he could no longer give the world Superman movies—but he had a chance to find meaning by using his celebrity to do things he valued, like serving as an active advocate for spinal cord injury patients and creating the Christopher Reeve Paralysis Foundation.

As evident from the story of Christopher Reeve, life events, no matter how difficult or challenging, are not as bleak as the cognitive distortion of catastrophic thinking makes one feel. Attacking depression in the face of significant life challenges and setbacks requires that you embrace the problem *as it is* (no matter how big, or how many) and stubbornly refuse to exaggerate the problem and its negative consequences. Attacking depression requires that you force yourself to focus on the "what is," not the "what could be" or the "what might be." It is important to challenge yourself to gain an accurate, realistic, and factual view of what is, the consequence experienced, and the possibilities of addressing those negative consequences.

These are not unbearable. The question is, therefore, not can you "bear" them but how do you choose to "bear" them? In attempting to stay focused on the reality of your experience, review your situation in light of the following questions.

1. What are the specific problems that I am CURRENTLY experiencing? List them. Write them down. Be sure that these are things you could point to if showing another.

2. For each challenge or problem, identify the specific impact it has on your life at this moment. What is it you can no longer do that you once did? What do you need to do now that is less than desirable, that you never had to do before? What are all the real negative and maybe even positive consequences of this situation?

3. Given the limitations or costs experienced as a result of this situation, what other things—things that you would have once felt were of value—can you still do or experience?

4. Given the list of specific impacts on your life, are there things you and/or others could do to reduce the costs or negative effects of these impacts?

Reviewing the details of the real problem and resisting the tendency to filter the problem through catastrophic filters will position you to (a) make the most of an undesirable situation, while at the same time (b) attempt to improve on the current situation.

Overgeneralization

One of the cognitive errors often exhibited by an individual who is depressed is overgeneralization. As described previously, overgeneralization is the cognitive distortion whereby an individual jumps to grand conclusions based upon a few or even a single event or experience. For those caught in the grips of depression, their focus shifts from the specific concerns to a perspective that defines their entire life as an unresolvable problem. With generalization as the filter through which to give meaning to life events, a job loss would be viewed as the announcement of the individual's life of poverty. Using generalization as a cognitive lens, the end of a meaningful relationship now is seen as evidence that the individual is unlovable and will spend the rest of their life alone. For those who are experiencing depression, the existence of mounting bills, gaining weight, or a diagnosis of a medical issue, when processed through the cognitive error of generalization, become "all too much to endure."

When attempting to defeat the "crazy" of overgeneralization, it is essential to identify and define the problems being experienced in very concrete terms. It is true that many individuals are confronted with many challenging circumstances. It is also true that regardless of the number of challenges, they are finite. It is essential to identify the specific issues and resist the tendency to group them all in one big, unresolvable mess. This point was brought home to me in a very creative and visual way by one of my clients.

I was able to work with one client who presented with severe depression and was actively engaged in both catastrophizing and overgeneralizing. Our time together was beneficial, and she was able to grow out of her depression. Months after we stopped working together, she dropped off a painting and a note, as a way of saying "Thank you." The picture was of a very…very…wrinkled elephant. At least that is what it looked like from a little distance. However, when you looked carefully at the picture, you discovered that it was actually made up of hundreds (my guess) of little mice all configured into the shape of an elephant. Her message was clear. Yes, she had many real problems and challenges, but when she was depressed, she wasn't seeing them as a finite number that could be addressed one at a time; instead, she was mentally clumping them all together (the elephant) in a way that made them too heavy to bear and genuinely unresolvable.

Selective Abstraction

I had a client who was a successful general surgeon. He was married to his childhood sweetheart, had three children (all in prestigious colleges), and all of the trappings of a financially successful life. Within his profession, he was seen as a truly gifted surgeon. He also served as a church elder and community leader. With this résumé, one might expect that he would be happy and self-satisfied. He was not. He was severely depressed.

The triggering event was his inability to save the life of a fourteen-year-old accident victim. The incident, however, served as only one element in the case he made against himself and which contributed to the maintenance of his depression. In our meetings, he would often report on his shortcoming as a physician, as a spouse, as a father, and as a man. While it could be argued that much of what he presented did provide evidence of his less-than-perfect performance as a physician, spouse, and even father, to dismiss his value as a person would require one to believe his "failures" were the total picture of his life. This is precisely what this client did. He was taking all of the experiences of his life, those supporting his successes and those indicating his failure, and focusing only on the negatives to the exclusion of the positives. With this selective abstraction of data, the reality he created was one in which he was not only a failure but would always be such a failure. It was this type of distorted reality that nourished his depression.

This process of attending to just some of the information while dismissing or discounting other data is an error that can result in one believing that one is worthless and the situation genuinely hopeless. Combating selective abstraction and its negative impact on your emotional well-being requires that you see "the whole picture," resisting the tendency to filter in or filter out specific information that you are using to draw your conclusions, about yourself, your life, or the world. Consider the following as steps to employ when engaged in selective abstraction.

1. Suspend your evaluation of the circumstances of

your life and simply list (describe) them as objective, factual events. For example, rather than saying "I was such a creep," simply describe the event, which in this case was "I told the waitress that I could have gone home and made my coffee in the time it took her to serve me."

2. Imagine that you shared the list that you just created with a close friend or family member. What other things (positive and negative) might they suggest you add to the list to make it complete?

For example, if you listed comments such as (a) failed to pay my bill on time; (b) refused to help my neighbor who was struggling with a flat tire; (c) yelled at my child for leaving his bike in the drive, your friend may have a couple of other insights. In reviewing your list the friend may add other negatives, for example, (a) yes, and you didn't repay the loan I gave you; and (b) you cursed at the older woman who was driving slowly. In addition your friend may note some positives, including (a) you picked me up when my car shut down; (b) you drive the kids, including mine, to all of their games and practices (when I can't); and (c) you offered to take care of our pets when we went on vacation.

3. Challenge yourself to identify one positive or even multiple positive elements that you would believe is evidence that you and your life are wonderful and always will be. I assume it is fair to suggest that you not only won't be able to find that evidence,

but it is likely you think the request was ridiculous. Well? I agree. So now, challenge yourself to identify the one negative—or, if you will, all of the negatives—that provides indisputable evidence that you and your life are horrible and hopeless and will be forever.

4. Review your list of negatives. First, for each negative identify a personal characteristic or an event and experience that you have had that would counterbalance that negative. For example, yes, you failed to help the neighbor with the tire, but you were available to watch their pets. Next, review the negatives you have listed and identify those for which you could take steps to eliminate or reduce if you wanted.

5. Review the entire list of negative and positive elements you have listed. Using the total picture as your reference point, is there any way you could rationally argue that your life is unbearable, that you are horrible, and that things are hopeless and helpless?

If you honestly engaged in the first four steps of data creation, then the answer to these questions found in step five would be no. The takeaway is that you need to stubbornly resist the temptation to engage in selective abstraction, seeing life through filters and distorting the total, real picture of you and your world.

Journaling Valuable in the Fight Against Depression

If you find that you have the energy needed to attack the cognitive distortions supporting your depression or down feelings, then return to the process of thought journaling. Specifically, whether you use a column approach or merely list things in order down the page, first identify the situations that you are defining as serving as the source of your depression. Next and most importantly, write down your self-talk, your interpretation, your belief or meaning that you are giving to this situation. With these as your data, now:

1. Examine the evidence
    Once your interpretations, your automatic thoughts, are identified, examine the facts. A complete review of the experience—identifying the "what is" while being sure to distinguish this from the "what could be" or "could have been"—will help reframe your interpretations so that they are reality based and functional.
2. Employ an alternate perspective
    Review the way you have interpreted the events that you have listed. Now, review the circumstances and your interpretation but imagine how you would respond to a friend who was offering that interpretation to that event. Or, if you prefer, attempt to identify how your friend or family member

would react if they saw how you were interpreting the event. Does this provide an alternative way of giving meaning to these events? If so—which perspective appears to be more factually supported? Which perspective, if either, seems to be reflecting cognitive distortions such as catastrophizing, generalization, or selective abstraction?

3. Black and white or gray?

If your self-talk reveals that you are processing the event through an either-or or all-or-nothing lens, challenge yourself by asking: (a) could it be or have been worse? (If so then it was not a catastrophe), and; (b) could it be better? (And as such this could be a goal for growth and thus not hopeless.)

4. Not YOU…IT

Something may be wrong. Perhaps you made a mistake, or in your view, you screwed up. This may be true, but it is IT that went wrong and not YOU. If your automatic thoughts suggest that you are labeling yourself with terms such as "loser," "idiot," "fool," etc., force yourself to define those terms. As you define the terms, ask yourself if you would apply these labels, with the same sense of personal devaluing, to a friend or family member who may have exhibited similar behavior or encountered a similar experience. Is it more accurate to label the behavior rather than the person? Did you "lose" at something? Did you act in ways you think were idiotic or foolish? It was the actions and situations deemed as less than desirable, not you.

5. Was it ALL you?

    When we are down on ourselves, the tendency is for us to take full, complete responsibility for all that went wrong. The goal is not to abdicate your involvement in the situation, but it is essential to challenge the blame you may be attributing to yourself if other things were involved. Is it possible that other forces were in play? Identify any other factors—other individuals or environmental conditions that contributed to the situation. Again, the goal is not to abdicate responsibility; actually, it is the exact opposite.

    By identifying all the forces involved, you will be positioned to take ownership of your part while at the same time considering ways to engage with the situation should it once again occur. This view will help you resist the tendency to believe it is hopeless and that you are helpless.

With a Little Help From...

When depressed it is possible that the very thought of fighting and attacking the depression may seem to be too much. Depression can exhaust you of all your resources, and it may be outside of your resources to defeat it. Believing that things are hopeless and that you are helpless can drain you of the energy and the motivation needed to engage in that attack. That is nothing to be ashamed of, and it is also no reason to conclude that it is hopeless.

Under these situations, it is essential that you reach out and contact a professional, a counselor, psychologist, psychiatrist, or clinical social worker who can help you at these times. If you are unaware of specialists or services in your area, consider talking with your family practitioner or local minister; often they will know those within the community who can help.

Connecting with a professional health care provider is not only the first step to overcoming your depression but is clear evidence of your resilience in engaging a problem-solving approach to this very painful experience. Congratulate yourself—you have not surrendered.

Epilogue: Slippers, Not Carpets

THERE ARE PEOPLE who buy into the big lie, that is the lie that directs them to believe that all of their emotional upset is the result of some external condition, and their path toward emotional well-being rests in making the world a nicer, more comforting, and more affirming place. For these individuals, their happiness and emotional well-being are often put on hold until they "reach retirement," "find that special someone," "avoid all bad news," or maybe "win the lottery." When the world is comfortable, they can be happy. It is as if they need all of life's rough spots to be carpeted over in order to protect their psychic "feet" and secure their emotional well-being.

That is sad. It is also unachievable and unnecessary.

Having come to the end of this book, you know that it is not in "carpeting" the world that one finds emotional comfort. Carpeting is not the answer since the world is not the problem. It is in clothing yourself in the "slippers" of rational thinking that you will be able to navigate all of the rough spots of life while supporting your emotional health and well-being.

You have hung in there and gotten to the end of this book. Congratulations! But this end is actually only the beginning.

While you now understand the pivotal role your thinking, your meaning-making plays in the creation and maintenance of your emotional well-being, it becomes your task to continue to develop a rational view of life, one that allows you to recognize the "crazies" of cognitive distortions and to reformulate your meaning-making so that it is rational and functional.

Just like the story of the little boy who stopped to ask a stranger, "How do I get to Carnegie Hall?" only to hear "Practice, practice, practice," that directive applies to you and me as we continue to defeat our crazies.

Rdp/2019

CPSIA information can be obtained
at www.ICGtesting.com
Printed in the USA
BVHW041929130320
575016BV00008B/45